# A Warrior's Guide To
# THE SEVEN SPIRITS OF GOD

## PART 1: BASIC TRAINING

**James A. Durham**

# TABLE OF CONTENTS

## APPENDICES

# FOREWARD

The night before I began to write the final draft of this book, I had a very vivid dream about a church staff preparing and conducting a dinner with a guest speaker. The program for the night was dealing with spiritual warfare. I saw each of the staff members busily making preparations and handling all the issues which arose. They seemed harried and often frustrated as detail after detail took their attention away from the program. There were so many problems which had to be resolved. After the dinner, the staff gathered before going home.

The leader said, "Now, that was some heavy spiritual warfare. The enemy was really opposed to us conducting this program and receiving this training! Others began to share all the difficulties they had faced that night and the challenges they had successfully met. The stories got bigger and more serious with each telling. At the end of their discussion, all felt very good. They had met the enemy, dealt with him, and came through it as victorious spiritual warriors.

Then I saw the enemy standing in one corner, and he seemed very pleased as well. He had kept the whole group distracted while he did his real work on the outside. He was not threatened by their dinner or the 45 minute lecture that followed. He knew that after a good night's sleep they would forget most of it, and the pressures of the next day would prevent them from employing what they had learned. In the meantime, 4,000 unborn children had been sacrificed through abortion to the modern day version of Molech. Drive by shootings had taken the lives of six youth. There were four murders in other parts of town. Countless numbers of drug deals had gone down on the streets of their city, and several teenagers had died from drug overdoses. There had been a major earthquake and many lives were lost, and the property damage was beyond calculating. A street riot had caused a great deal of damage to property as well as human lives. All in all, the enemy felt like it had been a very successful night of spiritual warfare.

I am convinced that spiritual warfare is being waged on a much grander scale than we have previously imagined. Battle lines have been drawn, and strongholds have been established. Unless we sharpen our skills at spiritual warfare and develop the gifts of discernment to new heights, we will not be making a significant impact on the world or in stemming the tide of the enemy's assault on us, our families, our churches, and our communities. We need the gift of spiritual discernment to recognize the real enemy, and to see the movement of the Holy Spirit in order to keep within the flow of God's anointing during these perilous times.

We have lost cities, states, and entire nations to the enemy's persistent drive to take territory and deny God access to the hearts and minds of the people. It is time to get off of the defensive and go on the offensive. It is time to take the battle to the enemy. It is time to execute well planned attacks on his strongholds, and win back the territory for the kingdom of God. To accomplish this, we need well trained, knowledgeable, and courageous spiritual warriors to take the point and lead the charge.

The purpose of this guidebook on spiritual warfare is to help these warriors see more clearly the resources provided by our Lord; to know the enemy and his tactics; to develop a strategy for responding to his attacks; and to move from defensive to offensive operations. We need to engage the enemy in his home territory and inflict maximum damage to his forces as we significantly hinder his tactical operations. Our goal is to take back God's people and His planet. Jesus came to destroy the works of the devil (1 John 3:8), and as His disciples, it is our task to carry on his work.

# ACKNOWLEDGEMENTS

There is never any real accomplishment purely through the work of one person. It is the Lord who gives us the ability and the inspiration to do His work; especially in the area of writing books about our faith, life, work, and calling. I want to give first priority to thanking the Lord for the inspiration and help I received in completing this work. To be honest, He deserves something over 99% of the credit.

I also want to acknowledge the amazing help I received from my blessed and anointed wife, Gloria. Without her inspiration, encouragement, and assistance this book could never have been completed. I also want to acknowledge my daughter, Michelle, who was a constant and consistent cheerleader throughout the process. When I had any misgivings, I had only to turn to either of these two wonderful ladies for encouragement and inspiration.

I am grateful to Pastor Huh, Chul, Pastor, Pal Bok Presbyterian Church in Chicago and the Pure Nard Publishing Company, for encouraging me to complete this work in a timely manner and for providing venues for me to engage in teaching these lessons to the valiant warriors who bravely go into battle daily to stand against the enemy and build the kingdom of God.

I would also like to express appreciation to many who have encouraged and supported me in the many months required to complete this project. I cannot mention all, but give a special word of gratitude to my wonderfully loyal daughter, Michelle; our spiritual daughters and ministry partners Maggie, Mia, MiSo, and Sookhee. I am also grateful to the members of Jesus Life Link Church in Seoul, Korea, Pastor Pi, Kee Young and Joshua Park for giving me the first opportunity to conduct this training in Korea and for their work in editing and publishing a student handbook for the training.

You have each been a blessing and inspiration to me and I will always be most grateful.

# INTRODUCTION

# "BEING READY FOR WAR"

In the book of Numbers, Chapter 1, God commanded Moses to take a census of all the people. This was not to determine the number of people traveling together on their way to the "promised land." This was a census to determine how many were able to fight in times of war.

> *"Now the Lord spoke to Moses in the Wilderness of Sinai, in the tabernacle of meeting, on the first day of the second month, in the second year after they had come out of the land of Egypt, saying: "Take a census of all the congregation of the children of Israel, by their families, by their fathers' houses, according to the number of names, every male individually, from twenty years old and above—all who are able to go to war in Israel. You and Aaron shall number them by their armies.* (Numbers 1:1-3)

For the purposes of this census, only the people able to go to war were included. To be eligible for war, you had to be a male 20 years of age or older. The Levites were not counted because even in wartime, their duties to minister unto the Lord took priority over fighting along with the army. They were to protect the Tabernacle and continue their priestly duties. In Numbers Chapter 1, we see the qualifier: "all who were ready to go to war" written down twelve separate times.

It is also important to notice that for the first time, God began to refer to the people as "armies." They had been elevated from a wandering group of former slaves to the status of the "armies of the Lord." God was literally speaking something into being. By His Word, they were being re-created, elevated, and empowered to accomplish His purpose. Following these decrees, the Lord began to train and equip the people for warfare. Some people today dislike this imagery of warfare and do not approve of viewing the Lord as the Commander in Chief. But Israel in the days of Moses understood it. In their circumstances, they recognized their need for a God who was a "man of war;" a God who would stand for them and defend them against enemies who came against them with trained and experienced military forces. After the Red Sea crossing and the defeat of Pharaoh's army, Moses and the people sang this song:

> *"Then Moses and the children of Israel sang this song to the LORD, and spoke, saying: "I will sing to the LORD, for He has triumphed gloriously! The horse and its rider He has thrown into the sea! The LORD is my strength and song, and He has become my salvation; He is my God, and I will praise Him; my father's God, and I will exalt Him. The LORD is a man of war; The LORD is His name. Pharaoh's chariots and his army He has cast into the sea; His chosen captains also are drowned in the Red Sea. The depths have covered them; they sank to the bottom like a stone. "Your right hand, O LORD, has become glorious in power; Your right hand, O LORD, has dashed the enemy in pieces."* (Exodus 15:1-6)

If we were asked by the Lord to take a census today of all the people who are ready and able to go to war, how many of our names would be on that list? How many of us are physically fit enough to enter battle? How many of us are mentally and spiritually strong enough to take a stand against the enemy? How many of us are willing to risk everything to obey the Lord's command? Do we have the mental toughness to be ready for war? When we consider these questions, we see more clearly our need to prepare ourselves in spirit, soul, and body to face an enemy who has already declared war against us. Are you ready?

Most people would rather have peace than war. This attitude is perfectly understandable. It is the right and righteous attitude which we should all possess. I assure you that no one wants peace more than someone who has endured the hardships and challenges of war. War is very expensive in terms of lives, money, and natural resources. War is painful and tends to traumatize those who get caught up in it. War is threatening, because we and our loved ones can lose our lives.

Having said this, I will also maintain that war is inevitable. There will always be power hungry men and women who will stop at nothing to have their own way and to establish themselves with position, authority and power. There will always be enemies who will emerge seeking to expand their area of ownership and control. This happens in the natural world, and it also happens in the spiritual realm. There is an enemy who is determined and focused on a purpose, and he has already declared war against us. Jesus says of this enemy, *"The thief does not come except to steal, and to kill, and to destroy."* (John 10:10) Peter restates these words and emphasizes the actions we must take to deal with him; *"Be sober, be vigilant; because your adversary the devil walks about like a roaring lion, seeking whom he may devour."* (1 Peter 5:8)

In the final analysis, we don't really have any choice about this war. When your enemy declares war against you, you are at war. It doesn't matter what you feel! It doesn't matter what you think! And, it doesn't matter what you want! The reality

*it began at salvation*

is that you are in a state of war. So, what are we supposed to do? In this regard, I have some good news. God has not left us without resources. God has not left us on our own to be weak and helpless victims standing against a powerful enemy. God has already sent help to support us in our cause.

*"And I looked, and behold, in the midst of the throne and of the four living creatures, and in the midst of the elders, stood a Lamb as though it had been slain, having seven horns and seven eyes, which are the seven Spirits of God sent out into all the earth."* (Revelation 5:6)

The Lord has sent out His seven Spirits to battle with us and for us. As you read Revelation 5:6, take note of all the "7s": 7 horns, 7 eyes, 7 spirits of God. Remember that seven is an important number in the Bible and in every prophetic utterance. The number seven means completeness or fullness. These seven Spirits provide all we need in our warfare with the devil. They are complete and represent all the power of God necessary for the church today.

## GIVEN THE FACT OF WAR, WHAT ARE WE SUPPOSED TO DO?

We need to know and understand our place in this conflict. We need to understand that we are not in charge, and we are not solely responsible for the outcomes. We are servants of the living God who is "a man of war," and He is fully capable of defeating the enemy on His own. But, He has decided to let us share in the victory so that we can stand firm in the peace of His kingdom when the battle is won. The first thing we should do is turn to scripture for comfort, encouragement and strength. Read aloud Psalm 121:1-8:

*I will lift up my eyes to the hills—From
whence comes my help?
My help comes from the LORD, Who made heaven and
earth.
He will not allow your foot to be moved; He who keeps
you will not slumber.
Behold, He who keeps Israel Shall neither slumber nor
sleep.
The LORD is your keeper; The LORD is your shade at
your right hand.
The sun shall not strike you by day, Nor the moon by
night.
The LORD shall preserve you from all evil; He shall
preserve your soul.
The LORD shall preserve your going out and your
coming in,
from this time forth, and even forevermore.*

We may always take courage in the sure knowledge that
we are not in this alone. God is with us. The Lord has sent
some powerful help to lead us on to victory. He has sent out the
seven Spirits of God into all the world.

It is important to note that these 7 Spirits are related to the
7 churches in the book of Revelation.

*"John, To the seven churches in the province of Asia:
Grace and peace to you from him who is, and who was,
and who is to come, and from the seven spirits before his
throne,"* (Revelation 1:4, NIV)

The seven Spirits which the Lord sent out and the seven
Spirits before the throne, are the same seven Spirits of God!
I believe that the seven churches mention by Jesus represent
the church age. They were real churches in that day, with real
issues and struggles. As we look at the challenges they faced,

we realize that these issues and struggles are common to all churches in all times. Everything which was happening in those churches is also happening to us now, in the church age. These seven letters from Jesus were sent in order to strengthen and prepare them for the warfare they were already engaged in at that time. These seven letters also apply to us in our current day warfare. And, the same message of encouragement and direction given by Jesus to them is equally relevant for us, today.

Many symbols and spiritual images are used to convey the full meaning of the messages to the church. Jesus uses angels, spirits, stars, lampstands, and eyes like flames of fire in order to communicate His message to the churches. These are all means Jesus uses to bless, strengthen, prepare, and discipline the church.

> *"To the angel of the church of Ephesus write, 'These things says He who holds the seven stars in His right hand, who walks in the midst of the seven golden lampstands':"* (Revelation 2:1)

Jesus is speaking to specific issues in these churches. At the end of each message, Jesus challenges those who have ears to hear and then He states that each message is for all the churches. Even in John's time, it was clear that the messages were for all churches wherever they might be located. And, remember, Jesus is also speaking to your church today. He is calling you to get ready for tribulation and warfare. I like the imagery of the seven stars. I like to think of Jesus as our Commander in Chief who is a Seven Star General.

In John's revelation, the seven spirits represent the awesome power of God, flowing through Jesus; through us; and into the world today.

> *"From the throne came flashes of lightning, rumblings and peals of thunder. Before the throne, seven lamps*

*were blazing. These are the seven spirits of God."*
(Revelation 4:5, NIV)

The really good news is that these seven amazingly powerful Spirits have been sent out to help us. As John was allowed to see them in this vision, they were not just twinkling or glowing, they were blazing with the power and glory of God. These Seven Spirits bring the awesome power of God into our circumstances. We are not alone! God is with us in His mighty power through these seven Spirits.

## WHAT ARE THESE SEVEN SPIRITS?

The church has often acted as if this is some great mystery which is yet to be revealed. I have listened to so many sermons saying we cannot know for sure the meaning of the Seven Spirits of God. I attended two theological seminaries, and this topic was never covered in class. In fact, I was told in one seminary not to study or preach this for at least the first 15 years of my ministry. The reason given for this injunction was to prevent bad preaching on the topics. I believed then and now that it was actually because they didn't feel qualified to teach about the true meaning of this book of the Bible.

It is important to remember that in the New Testament a mystery is something formerly hidden which has now been made known. By this definition of mystery — The understanding of the seven Spirits of God has been made known. So the real question is: "Why don't we know it?"

The Bible has revealed and identified a number of different spirits. Some of the names of these spirits are very humorous. For example we read about a spirit of stupor in chapter 11 of the book of Romans. That always reminds me of Jesse Duplantis joking about a spirit of stupid coming over people. The Bible also talks about people having a spirit of dizziness, and that can be taken two ways (actual or intellectual dizziness). We also read about a spirit of the world, a spirit of judgment, a spirit of infirmity, and etc.

I did a computer search of the entire Bible to find all the references to the phrase "spirit of." In the New King James Version, there are at least 122 references to the "spirit of........" Some are spirits sent by God: i.e. spirit of faith, unity, etc. Others are demonic spirits sent by the enemy.

In the English versions of the Bible, some of the Spirits are translated using a capital "S" in the word Spirit. This indicates that the translators viewed this particular Spirit as a function of God or more precisely as the Holy Spirit. When I was considering this, I thought, "Wouldn't be interesting if there were exactly seven of these spirits revealed with a capitol 'S'?" In my computer search, I found precisely seven different "Spirits of." The seven Spirits so <u>identified</u> are:

**1. The Spirit of wisdom and revelation (prophesy)**

**2. The Spirit of truth**

**3. The Spirit of holiness**

**4. The Spirit of life**

**5. The Spirit of sonship (adoption)**

**6. The Spirit of grace**

**7. The Spirit of glory**

It became my conviction that these are the seven spirits of God sent out into all the world by our Lord, Jesus. These seven powerful spirits bring all of the power, wisdom, grace, glory, and righteousness we need to deal with our ancient enemy, the devil.

I also recognized from scripture and my own experience after more than 43 years in the ministry that every time these spirits begin to operate in our lives or in the church, the enemy responds. It is the enemy's strategy to win a victory by stopping or at least hindering the work of the Holy Spirit in the church. I believe that the enemy also operates through seven powerful unholy spirits which are also call principalities. They are referred to as principalities because each has a prince demon in authority over it

*"Then another sign appeared in heaven: an enormous red dragon with seven heads and ten horns and seven crowns on his heads. His tail swept a third of the stars out of the sky and flung them to the earth. The dragon stood in front of the woman who was about to give birth, so that he might devour her child the moment it was born."* (Revelation 12:3, NIV)

I believe that these seven heads with seven crowns are prince demons who are over the enemy's principalities on earth. In Ephesians chapter 6, Paul said that our struggle is not against flesh and blood, but against principalities and powers. These seven principalities and their subordinate demons and spirits have worked through people to accomplish the enemy's purpose all through human history. The people who first exhibit these demons die, but the demon spirits do not die. They will still be alive when they join the Antichrist and the false prophet in the Lake of Fire after the final judgment. In the meantime, they and their subordinate demons still work through people today. They are very deceptive. So, we must stay on guard to avoid deception.

The enemy always uses one or both of his two primary tactics in dealing with the church. His first tactic is to send in counterfeit spirits. At first, they look and feel like the real thing, but if you go along with these enemy spirits, things begin to go wrong; things just don't work right. They have been sent to accomplish the enemy's purpose which we have already seen is to steal your blessing and your anointing, to kill you hopes and your dreams (perhaps your body as well), and to destroy your work for the Lord and your influence in the world.

If a spirit is truly from the Lord — if it is the Spirit of God, it will bring positive change! It will bring renewal. It will bring refreshing. A Spirit from God will take you from glory to glory. It will bring the blessings and protection of the Lord into your life and your situation. But if it is one of those counterfeit spirits, it is going to attempt to block or hinder every work of God in your life and in your ministry. It will constantly be taking you on a downward spiral to ultimate failure. So, we must be alert and watchful. We need to seek most of all the spiritual gift of discernment to face the challenges of spiritual warfare in our world today.

The Second Tactic which the enemy likes to use is to launch a direct frontal assault on us designed to draw our attention away from God and away from God's Spirits. For example, if he launches an attack, you may quit focusing on the Spirit of life working in you or your church, you may begin to focus on the bad things that are happening. You may get caught up in dealing with the hurt you are experiencing. Your full attention may be directed to the problems which are occurring instead of the blessings the Lord is providing for you to overcome these attacks. I have seen this work over and over, and I believe that you have also seen this happen.

It is crucially important to remember that the enemy is "anti" or against the work of Christ. Remember how John described his work in his first epistle.

*"...every spirit that does not confess that Jesus Christ has come in the flesh is not of God. And this is the spirit of the Antichrist, which you have heard was coming, and is now already in the world." (1 John 4:3)*

Please note that this is the "spirit of the antichrist," and not the Antichrist. The Antichrist has not yet been revealed, but the spirit of antichrist is already in the world doing his dirty work. Christ came to destroy the works of the devil.

*"For this purpose the Son of God was manifested, that He might destroy the works of the devil."* (1 John 3:8b)

Satan's response to the work of God in our lives is to try to destroy the work of Jesus. What did Jesus say was the devil's purpose? *"The thief does not come except to steal, and to kill, and to destroy."* (John 10:10) Every time one of these seven Spirits of God begins to work in your life or in the church, the enemy will come, and he will try to stop it.

The enemy's most destructive and unfortunately his most successful plan is to use people on the inside of your church group to do his dirty work. You need to learn some important lessons from the history of warfare in the world. Virtually every successful military leader has learned to follow the 9 principles of war (See Appendix A: Carl Von Clausewitz: 9 Principles of War). When you study the 9 principles of war, you will discover that one of them is called, "Security." The key task is to keep the enemy outside the camp, because normally you fight back to back, shooting at the enemy from whatever direction he attacks. But, if the enemy is inside the camp, and you turn to fire on the enemy, you wind up shooting each other. So, when the enemy gets inside the camp, you will begin to inflict casualties on your own forces.

The Bible is full of examples of this type of enemy activity.

a. Example: Judas - at the last supper when Jesus was instituting this celebration as a fulfillment of the Passover feast, the spirit of Satan came right into Judas. He was inside the group, and then he turned against Jesus and the entire group of disciples. Notice: this happened at a high point of Jesus' time with the disciples. And it can happen to us when we are moving into something powerful for the Lord.

b. Then look at what happened to Peter just a few hours later. Jesus told Peter that before the night was over, he would deny Him three times. Peter said, "Never! Not even death could make this happen." He didn't trust what Jesus had said to warn him. He didn't believe that he could become a victim of the enemy's plan. Then we see that Satan came in, and from within the camp he damaged the disciples through what Peter did.

We must remain aware that every time one or more of these seven Spirits begins to work in the church, the enemy moves in to block it. When we see people fall, we may look down on them and even attempt to shame them. We look at Peter, Judas, Thomas and say, "How could they do that to the Lord and to their fellow disciples? However, even as we're still talking about this, the enemy moves right in, and uses one of us to attack the church from the inside. He always finds someone in the group whom he can use against the group. He is looking for someone who will begin to question what's happening in the body of Christ. He wants to find someone who is vulnerable and will begin to whisper things about other people in the group. This quickly turns into gossip, and lives are damaged or destroyed in the process. *So true*

Now, I want you to catch this. When this happens in your group (family or church), you wonder, "How could anyone turn and do something like this after being warned?" We must never lose sight of the fact that each and every one of us is at risk. Jesus warned Peter that he would deny Him that night, but Peter didn't believe it could happen to him. When we believe it can't happen to us, we are at risk. The reality is that it happens over and over again in the church. Unless you prepare yourself, the enemy will be successful against you too. He gets away with doing it over and over, and each time we are surprised and shocked.

I believe the power of the church today has been broken by the enemy's success at getting someone inside the group to turn against the church and cause a split. Instead of growing in power, we are broken in pieces from within.

We see the enemy's work in the seven churches in Revelation. Again, we must remember that these churches represent the present age; the church age. They stand as an awesome reminder of what the enemy can do in our churches today. Only one of the seven churches was doing everything right. Six of them were having serious problems with demonic spirits working against the body of Christ. In some of them, they were knowingly tolerating these enemy spirits.

These seven churches stand before us as an awesome reminder of the enemy's plan, his ability to deceive, and his ability to succeed when the church is not vigilant. He does it over and over again, and gets away with it. How can this be? How can we be fooled over and over? I believe that it is because his greatest deception is to keep it all hidden from view. He has been successful at making people think that it's just not real. It doesn't really happen, and if it does, it couldn't happen to us.

In today's world, if you go around talking about spirits and demons, what happens to you? Someone will say it's time for some mental health treatment or hospitalization. The greatest deception in the world is Satan's success in getting educated people in influential positions to believe that he doesn't exist, and that demons are not real. When demon possessed or oppressed people believe this, the demons can operate freely. No one is watching them! No one is prepared to deal with them or to confront them.

The Bible tells us that one third of all the angels in heaven fell with Satan and became demon spirits. Think about it! Satan turned one third of the angels against God from within the camp. How many is that? John saw 10,000 X 10,000 and thousands of thousands of angels in heaven. So, if half of that number were expelled, that is a very large number. They are here among us and they are operating against us. We are at war! We are enmeshed in spiritual warfare whether we like it or not.

## SO, HOW DO YOU PREPARE FOR SPIRITUAL WARFARE?

We can learn from the experiences of military forces throughout history. There are specific techniques and strategies which are common to all warfare. We can apply these techniques and strategies to the spiritual warfare we're in now. Special Forces and SWAT teams have learned to employ special weapons and tactics in their operations. We need to do the same as we develop Special Forces units in the body of Christ. We must learn to employ the special weapons which the Lord has prepared for us.

*"For though we walk in the flesh, we do not war according to the flesh. For the weapons of our warfare are not carnal but mighty in God for pulling down strongholds, casting down arguments and every high thing that exalts itself against the knowledge of God, bringing every thought into captivity to the obedience of Christ, and being ready to punish all disobedience when your obedience is fulfilled."* (2 Corinthians 10:3-6)

So what are these weapons? The prophet Zechariah was given great insight into this question in his vision of the lamp-stand.

*"Now the angel who talked with me came back and wakened me, as a man who is wakened out of his sleep. And he said to me, "What do you see?" So I said, "I*

*am looking, and there is a lampstand of solid gold with a bowl on top of it, and on the stand seven lamps with seven pipes to the seven lamps. Two olive trees are by it, one at the right of the bowl and the other at its left." So I answered and spoke to the angel who talked with me, saying, "What are these, my lord?" Then the angel who talked with me answered and said to me, "Do you not know what these are?" And I said, "No, my lord." So he answered and said to me: "This is the word of the Lord to Zerubbabel: 'Not by might nor by power, but by My Spirit,' Says the Lord of hosts."* (Zechariah 4:1-6)

Again, did you notice all of the number sevens? There were seven lamps, and seven pipes. The angel explains these as the Spirit of the Lord. Now, we are right back to the seven Spirits of God. These seven Spirits of God are our special warfare weapons.

Is anyone ready to sign up for God's Special Forces? Are you ready to be issued some special weapons and given some new tactics? Are you ready to stop losing and start winning? Do you want to be the ones who think outside the box and constantly surprise the enemy? Do you want to let the enemy deal with shock and awe instead of constantly being surprised by him? It's time for us to get off the defensive and go on the offensive. If we're going to be engaged in that kind of spiritual warfare, we have to be on the alert and be wise. Jesus said, *"Behold, I send you out as sheep in the midst of wolves. Therefore be wise as serpents and harmless as doves."* (Matthew 10:16) *Pigs love to get dirty, sheep don't like the mud*

To be fully prepared for spiritual warfare, we need to be trained on the weapons of our warfare. The primary purpose of this book is to provide this training for you and your church.

The first step you must take is to educate yourselves, then to remain alert and aware. You need to take to heart Peter's words in His first letter:

*"Beloved, do not think it strange concerning the fiery trial which is to try you, as though some strange thing happened to you; but rejoice to the extent that you partake of Christ's sufferings, that when His glory is revealed, you may also be glad with exceeding joy. If you are reproached for the name of Christ, blessed are you, for the Spirit of glory and of God rests upon you. On their part He is blasphemed, but on your part He is glorified."* (1 Peter 4:12-14)

From the passages of scripture you will study in this training, you will see one important guarantee: When the Spirit of glory rests on you, the enemy is going to come after you! The enemy hates the glory, and he wants to destroy it. Peter knew what he was talking about when he wrote this. I have an idea that the day Peter wrote this he was remembering when Jesus said: "Simon, Simon, Satan has asked to sift you as wheat." (Luke 22:31) Can you picture that? Can you image the tone in Jesus' voice when he said, *"Simon, Simon..."* Can you picture Satan going up to God and saying, "I'd like to sift old Peter like wheat. You know that he doesn't have the right stuff. He's never going to make a good disciple, and I'm going to sift him right out of the group. Can I have permission to do that?" He actually asked God to let him do that to Peter! He didn't get away with it, but he certainly tried. Why? What stopped him from sifting Peter? It was because Jesus prayed for Peter, and God listened to Jesus.

So, How do we repeatedly get surprised by the enemy's attacks? Peter didn't think it could happen to him. He said, "No, no, Lord! That can't happen to me! Even to death I will stand by you!" And, yet before the night was over, he did it. I think Peter was genuinely surprised by his own actions. And, he wrote these words out of that painful experience. It happens because we don't stay alert and because we are unaware of the enemy's methods and means. When we are not aware of these factors, we are vulnerable to the enemy's attacks in our lives. Remember Paul's warning to Timothy:

> *"So I counsel younger widows to marry, to have children, to manage their homes and to give the enemy no opportunity for slander. Some have in fact already turned away to follow Satan."* (1 Timothy 5:14-15, NIV)

The part of this passage I want you to understand is the warning: "give the enemy no opportunity." Can you imagine that? Some people in the body of Christ had already turned away to follow Satan. Paul makes it clear that we have to be very, very careful not to give the enemy any opportunity. This is crucially important for us to understand, because the veil of deception comes so slowly; so quietly; and so gently to cover our spiritual eyes. It normally comes with a few seemingly harmless questions. Remember how Satan approached Jesus. He first said, *"If you really are the Son of God?"* He wanted to erode Jesus' confidence in His calling, His relationship with the Father, and His ultimate victory. And he wants to do that to you as well. So, he comes at you with these little doubt-filled questions to slowly erode your confidence. He asks questions like:

Do you really think you are the child of God?

Do you really believe that stuff?

Come on now! Get serious!

Do you think God really loves you?

Do you really think God has forgiven all the mistakes in your past?

The enemy always comes with sneaky little questions like these trying to erode our confidence and plant doubt in us. If you start listening to these things (paying attention to what he's saying) you are on a slippery slope down a steep hill. Remember what Paul said to the church at Ephesus, *"and do not give the devil a foothold."* (Ephesians 4:27 - NIV) Several years ago many companies in the United States primarily sold their products door to door. Some of you may remember the Electrolux salesmen. They would stick their foot into the door so you couldn't close it. Some of them would throw dirt through the opening so you would have to let them come in and vacuum up the mess. Eventually everyone knew not to let a salesman get his foot in the door! They knew better than to give him a foothold. We need to deal with the enemy the same way. Don't let him get his foot in the door. Don't even let him have a foot on the steps of your house! Resist the devil and he will flee! Right?

> *"Therefore submit to God. Resist the devil and he will flee from you."* (James 4:7)

You must resist him! You must stand against him, because Satan wants to get you into a battle of wits. And, He does it with those little questions. Don't start reasoning with him. He has had lots of practice and he's good at it. He knows the answers to almost everything you can say. So don't argue with him! He will outwit you. Don't try to reason with the enemy! Do what Jesus did. Stay in the Word of God. Quote the Word to him. And most importantly live in accordance with the Word. One of the places he gets to so many believers is in the area of unforgiveness. You need to heed Paul's instructions:

*"If you forgive anyone, I also forgive him. And what I have forgiven—if there was anything to forgive –* [I like this: "If there was anything to forgive. Very often we get offended by things we thought someone said or things we thought they did, and they did not intend it that way at all. So if there really is anything to forgive...] *— I have forgiven in the sight of Christ for your sake, in order that Satan might not outwit us. For we are not unaware of his schemes."* (2 Corinthians 2:10-11, NIV)

This is one of those subtle little places where you can give him a foothold. When you don't forgive others, you have opened the door for the enemy to attack you, outwit you, and oppress you. But you are aware! You do know that unless you forgive, you are not forgiven, because with the same measure that you measure out judgment, it will be measured out to you. To get forgiveness, you have to give it. Do what Jesus did: even on the cross, he forgave those who treated him with such hatred and contempt. He forgave those who were in the process of killing Him. You need to be like that! Otherwise you give Satan a foothold. Otherwise you set yourself up to be outwitted by him.

What you need to do is stand in the authority and stand in the power of God. You need to live in the power and authority He has given to all believers. You must stand in that power! You must stand in that authority! You need to stand up to the enemy. Make this confession: "I submit to God and I resist the Devil and he must flee from me." Amen? As Paul said to his spiritual son Timothy, *"For God did not give us a spirit of timidity, but a spirit of power, of love and of self–discipline."* (2 Timothy 1:7, NIV)

The church is acting so timidly in the world today! Christians are tiptoeing around; making sure they don't say anything politically incorrect; making sure they don't offend anyone; and making sure everyone feels good. In doing this, we have picked up this spirit of timidity! Did that come from God? Absolutely not! God did not give you a spirit of timidity, but of power, of love, and of self-discipline, and you need to begin to act like it.

**WARNING**: If you do this, the enemy will come against you.

If you begin to study this and start operating in accordance with God's Word, the enemy will come after you! However, do not be afraid! The Lord is with you and will provide all you need to deal with the enemy. Additionally, you need to be aware that the enemy will come against you whether you are aware of his tactics or not. He will come against you whether you fight or not. It is much better to be aware and prepared.

What he will try to do is come after you from the inside using someone close to you. He will try to come at you in your marriage relationship, and in your family. He will come at you in the body of Christ. He will come at you somewhere from the inside.

1). He will find somebody who has left the door of his heart open.

2). He will find somebody who is vulnerable to his questions.

3). He'll find somebody and begin to stir it up on the inside.

But, know this for sure, he will come against you. Don't back down! Use the weapons God provides: the seven Spirits of God!

The remainder of this book will focus on spiritual warfare. We have been called to God's Special Forces! We have been called to active duty. The question is: Are you ready to report for active duty? If you are, you need to know that the reason you are on active duty is because there is a real enemy. You get called to active duty when there is a war. You may not have declared war, but the enemy did. And, I want to tell you again that when your enemy declares war, you are at war whether you like it or not. We are in spiritual warfare. You have been called to active duty to be a part of God's powerful end-times army. In the next few lessons, you will go through spiritual boot camp and after boot camp you may choose to go through Advanced Individual Training (AIT) which is covered in the next book of this series.

ARE YOU READY? Are you ready for spiritual boot camp? [Hoo-ah!]

In these lessons, you are going to learn <u>HOW</u> to stand against the enemy. You will learn about the many ways the enemy may come against you. One important KEY to dealing with the enemy is to know that he is not creative. When you study the scripture in these lessons, you will see that the enemy keeps coming at you in the same seven areas. When God begins to flow in a particular area of your life through one of the seven Spirits, the enemy will come at you in the same area. When the Lord begins to manifest His presence in your ministry through one of the seven Spirits, the enemy will come against your ministry in that same area. So, be prepared! Don't be surprised!

Paul's challenge to the Ephesian church is still our challenge today, *"when you have done everything to stand, STAND!"* You know that your battle is not against flesh and blood. It is against principalities and powers, against spiritual forces of darkness in heavenly places. The only way you are going to be able to stand is to put on the whole armor of God. Do you realize that there are seven pieces of that armor? Could this possibly be prophetic? There are seven Spirits sent throughout the world; there are seven enemy spirits that come against it, and there are seven pieces of armor. So, as you study these seven Spirits of God, you will learn how the enemy comes against us, and what you need to do to overcome.

Prepare yourself! While we are doing this, expect an attack — usually from someone on the inside. Expect the enemy to come. When you are prepared, you don't fall into the same old traps. You will learn to quickly say, "Aha! I caught you! I see what you are up to! I'm not going to fall for that! I'm not going to get into a fight with my spouse! I'm not going to let myself get involved in grumbling and arguing in the church! I'm not going to be the person who gets led into doubt, and gets into shame! I'm not going to do that! I'm standing with Jesus, because Jesus has released the power and authority for me to do that!" Amen?

## PRAYER OF SUBMISSION TO GOD
## TO GET READY FOR BATTLE.

Father God, we submit to you in spirit, soul, and body; all we are and all we ever hope to be; all we have and all we ever hope to have, and we resist the devil. In accordance with your Word and in the Mighty name of Jesus, he must flee and take all his works with him. And, Lord God we ask your help as we stand in against the enemy in the power and authority you have given to us. We ask for all seven of those Spirits to be sent out by Jesus to operate in our church, in our families, and in our lives. We ask your help to have the courage to stand. We are putting on the spiritual armor! We stand against the enemy! We trust your Word! We trust that he will flee when we stand, and we decree that when we have done everything to stand, we will keep on standing in faith and in Jesus Christ.

Father God, we thank you for sending power into the body of Christ! We thank you that you send power into our lives, Lord God, and we want to use that power for your kingdom. Lord God, we are just sold out to you! As we submit to you, we are giving you everything we have, and there is nothing left for the enemy. So, we declare to the enemy, "You might as well pack your bags and hit the road, make your way back to the pit, because we are standing in agreement and in the mighty power of God. You can do no further harm to us. We are going to stand together, and be bound together as the Lord's Special Forces. We stand in His glorious name and for your kingdom. Lord God, be with us as we pray in the glorious name of Yeshua ha Messiach! Amen and Amen!

I want to end this lesson with a promise: *"Yet the Lord is faithful, and he will strengthen you and set you on a firm foundation and guard you from the evil one."* (2 Thessalonians 3:3, AMP)

## NOTES

# LESSON 1

# "THE SPIRIT OF PROPHECY"

I have a message for you from our Commander in Chief, the one and only Seven Star General, Jesus Christ, King of kings and Lord of lords.

> *"Or suppose a king is about to go to war against another king. Will he not first sit down and consider whether he is able with ten thousand men to oppose the one coming against him with twenty thousand? If he is not able, he will send a delegation while the other is still a long way off and will ask for terms of peace."* (Luke 14:31-32, NIV)

Welcome to the first lesson of spiritual boot-camp!

When I was on active duty as a chaplain, boot-camp lasted seven weeks. As I received the inspiration from the Lord to prepare this study, I was somewhat surprised to realize that the study of the seven Spirits would take the same amount of time. Spiritual boot-camp is best divided into seven sessions which are intended to be done in seven weeks of training. Taking a full week to study, absorb and process the teaching will greatly enhance your understanding and help you to develop skills at handling the appropriate tasks which go along with each session. It is amazing how prophetic many things in the military are to the spirit realm (or perhaps it is the other way around).

I would like to start by saying, "Ladies and gentlemen, WE ARE AT WAR!"

Our enemy has declared war and he is attacking relentlessly. Moment by moment, day by day the enemy is on the offensive. His objectives are clear: he would like to annihilate each and every one of you. That is his purpose. So, I have another word from our Commander in Chief (CINC).

*"The thief does not come except to steal, and to kill, and to destroy. I have come that they may have life, and that they may have it more abundantly."* (John 10:10)

Based on the Word of God, you know that the enemy's objective is to steal, kill, and destroy. So, in order for you to survive, you must learn how to correctly wage spiritual warfare. To enhance your survivability, you need to learn basic tactical procedures; become familiar with your weapons; and develop proficiency is maintaining and firing these highly technical and exceptionally powerful weapons. As in regular military basic training, you must train and qualify on spiritual weapons of warfare.

You need to learn survival skills to not only endure the extremes of climate and terrain, but to protect and preserve the strength of your fighting force. In military training it is necessary to learn first aide. In combat situations, medical help is not always immediately available and soldiers must learn how to bind up wounds, stop bleeding, administer pain medications, and splint broken limbs. In spiritual warfare, you also need to know how to bandage the wounded. Spiritual wounds vary, but are usually as painful and debilitating as physical wounds. You must learn how to bind up the brokenhearted and restore each other in order to keep up your fighting capability. Jesus declared that the promise in Isaiah 61 was a description of His ministry and therefore of our ministry as His disciples.

> *"The Spirit of the Lord God is upon Me, because the Lord has anointed Me to preach good tidings to the poor; He has sent Me to heal the brokenhearted, to proclaim liberty to the captives, and the opening of the prison to those who are bound; To proclaim the acceptable year of the Lord, and the day of vengeance of our God; To comfort all who mourn, to console those who mourn in Zion, to give them beauty for ashes, the oil of joy for mourning, the garment of praise for the spirit of heaviness; that they may be called trees of righteousness, the planting of the Lord, that He may be glorified."*
> (Isaiah 61:1-3)

In addition to training on your weapons and developing your survival skills, you must also study the enemy's tactics, weapons, and capabilities. You need to know how he operates, so that you can prepare your defenses against his operational skills.

Most of the areas you have addressed in the past most likely have to do with defensive measures. However to achieved victory you must learn how to take the offensive. This is one of the nine principles of war which you must learn to employ in order to achieve your tactical objectives. For too long, the church has been in a defensive posture, and we have watched the enemy repeatedly attack and take people and resources from us. We have been letting him win a war of attrition. To turn this around, we need to know how to go on the offensive and take the battle to him. When we take the initiative we can get another principle of war working for us. This principle is the element of surprise. Offensive operations are the only effective method of controlling the element of surprise. When you take the offensive you give the enemy an opportunity to

*give me understanding - How!*

experience "shock and awe" personally. It is time for a major counter offensive on our part.

To establish a level of combat readiness, you must develop skills at staying alert and on guard. So many churches lose their effectiveness because they allow enemy spirits to come in, and they tolerate the disruptive behavior of those who are oppressed by the enemy. We have repeatedly failed in the area of security. On guard duty, soldiers learn the 10 general orders. All of these orders have to do with how you secure your post; how you maintain security; how you observe for enemy movement (attacks and infiltration); and how you sound the alarm to alert the rest of your forces. Soldiers quickly learn that they must establish and maintain security in their assigned area of operation. Like good soldiers on active duty wanting to please your commander, you must stay awake, alert, and on guard against enemy movement.

Remember that there are two basic ways an enemy comes against you. The enemy will either make a strait on attack or attempt to infiltrate your area. So, you have to make sure that you don't go to sleep on guard duty! In wartime, going to sleep on guard duty can result in capital punishment. This is serious business. You absolutely must to stay alert in wartime, and we are at war spiritually all the time. Remember how many times Jesus told his disciples to keep watch, stay on the alert, and be ready at all times.

Our basic scriptural text for this entire training is:

*"And I looked, and behold, in the midst of the throne and of the four living creatures, and in the midst of the elders, stood a Lamb as though it had been slain, having seven horns and seven eyes, which are the seven Spirits of God sent out into all the earth."* (Revelation 5:6)

These Seven Spirits were sent out into all the earth to help us in our warfare against the devil. Jesus sent them out to fight with us and for us. They are the awesome representatives of our friendly forces from the Lord.

In any military operation, you need to know who you are dealing with. To accomplish this, you must conduct a thorough analysis of the enemy situation and strength. At the same time, you also need to know who is on your side. In other words, you need to know the makeup of your friendly forces. God sent the Holy Spirit, as the ultimate friendly force, to give you the kind of strength you need to stand.

Once again, I want you to know the danger you face when you decide to operate in the prophetic. To be properly prepared to deal with the danger, you need to accomplish some basic tasks. First, begin by valuing very highly what God has entrusted to you. Next, be faithful in the use of every resource provided by the Lord. Then, be faithful to inspire and pass on what you have learned to the next generation. The next generation is always being prepared to take up the fight and continue where you left off.

> *"Guard the good deposit that was entrusted to you— guard it with the help of the Holy Spirit who lives in us."* (2 Timothy 1:14, NIV)

God will provide you with the power you need to accomplish your purpose. That is the "good deposit" He has entrusted to you. He said He would send the Holy Spirit, and He is faithful. In fact, He has already done it.

> *"But you shall receive power when the Holy Spirit has come upon you; and you shall be witnesses to Me in Jerusalem, and in all Judea and Samaria, and to the end of the earth."* (Acts 1:8)

Many people read this passage (even in church), but they don't really believe that there is real power available for the

*help me understand* all involved in this power.

church today. They believe that all of this was for the first century church and is no longer available to us. But Jesus said, *"You are going to receive power!"* and I think you should trust His word. You should expect to receive power. And, you should be receiving it and living in that power, because you need it for the war you are in right now.

So, the purpose of these seven spirits is to bring power to bear in your life. This is what you want to do when you go to war. You want to bring strategic power against the enemy. You want to have air superiority so you can freely fly through the enemy's area of operation, bomb them, fire on them, and continue to resupply your own troops. You want to have superiority on the seas so you can fire those big guns on enemy positions from a safe distance away. You want to have artillery superiority so you can bring devastating fire power on the enemy.

If you have ever been at war or seen a fire power demonstration, you know that the weapons being fired provide an absolutely devastating force. The ground shakes. It is like the description in the Bible: When God comes, the mountains quake and the earth shakes from the power of God moving into the area. In wartime, when the big guns fire and the bombs explode, you can literally feel the earth shaking. Great power is released in warfare.

In spiritual warfare, you will also be releasing great power. In the church and at conferences, we talk about taking the nations (taking the gospel to the nations and winning entire countries for the Lord), but I want to tell you that it is only when you begin to operate in the power of the Holy Spirit that you even have a chance of taking it to the nations.

From ancient times, God promised to send a very special gift of the Spirit. He promised from hundreds; maybe thousands of years ago that He was going to send the spirit of prophecy:

*"There shall come forth a Rod from the stem of Jesse, And a Branch shall grow out of his roots. The Spirit of the Lord shall rest upon Him, The Spirit of wisdom and understanding, The Spirit of counsel and might, The Spirit of knowledge and of the fear of the Lord."* (Isaiah 11:1-2)

That same Spirit of the Lord which was prophesied to come on Jesus can also come on you. God wants you to walk in the same way Jesus walked. Jesus was not some super human which none of us will ever be able to imitate. In terms of His relationship with God and His eternal power, we will never attain to the fullness of that. But, the way He lived on earth and the things He did here are a model for you to grow into and live up to. If you are filled with the Holy Spirit and operating in the power of the Holy Spirit, you should be experiencing what Jesus declared, "Not only will you do the things I have done, but even greater things than these." The problem is that we have not walked in that fullness. However, you are told in Scripture that you are supposed to be walking in that level of power and authority. Much of this is only realized fully when you receive the Spirit of prophecy. This Spirit is such a major part of the fulfillment of God's promise.

Centuries after Isaiah prophesied the coming of this Spirit, Paul referred it as the Spirit of Wisdom and Revelation.

*"I keep asking that the God of our Lord Jesus Christ, the glorious Father, may give you the Spirit of wisdom and revelation, so that you may know him better."* (Ephesians 1:17, NIV)

confess - give evidence of

I highly recommend that you read, study, and memorize this entire section in Ephesians Chapter 1. As you study it, notice that there are several other things that come after this passage which Paul attributes to the working of this Spirit in your life. I

profess: to say that you are, do, or feel something when other people don't what you say.

43

recommend for you to read this regularly to make the promise yours. Make this your prayer as you sincerely ask the Lord to give you the Spirit of wisdom and revelation. Remember the promise of Jesus recorded in Luke 11:13, *"If you then, being evil, know how to give good gifts to your children, how much more will your heavenly Father give the Holy Spirit to those who ask Him!"*

During his visit to the third heaven, an angel told John that this is the spirit of prophecy. Revelation 19:10, *"For the testimony of Jesus is the spirit of prophecy."* In this training session, as you study the work of this Spirit of God in the church and in us, I will be referring to it most often as the Spirit of prophecy.

## TO SURVIVE IN WARFARE, YOU NEED THE SPIRIT OF PROPHECY!

I know from painful experience what can happen to people who choose to preach or teach on this topic. I have known people who got up to preach and couldn't speak that day. Their throat would literally shut. I've known people who have become ill and could not go to the church to preach. And, I've known people who have come under great attack for talking about what we are going to talk about in this session.

The first time I preached on this, I prayed for God to give me boldness to speak and strength to stand. As I continued to pray during the time of praise and worship, the Lord let me see a row of angels standing behind the pulpit, and renewed strength filled me in spirit, soul, and body. Twice my throat became soar and I had difficulty talking before the training. I broke it off by continuously confessing that "by His stripes I was healed." Because I have experienced attacks, I always ask a congregation or class of students to pray with me that I may be able to teach these things properly and speak boldly and in truth. This is a very important topic, and it is very serious business. For this reason, the enemy will try to hinder or block you from knowing some of these things. Don't give up and don' give in! God is infinitely more powerful than the enemy. Stand on His promises!

In the past, so many people have done church business as if it were a kind of children's "play church." They have approached the business of the church like children playing a very simple game. They want to learn the simple rules, play the game, and have a great deal of fun every time they play. People with this attitude are likely to see the church as primarily a source of entertainment and amusement. When they are challenged to take a stand for the Lord or they are faced with difficult times they tend to fall away. The fear of losing members is the driving force behind the "seeker sensitive" church model which avoids anything unpleasant or challenging. However, real church is for true disciples who love the Lord more than they love their own lives. They don't hide from spiritual warfare, but like the champions in David's army, they run to the sound of battle ready to fight the good fight of faith. It is important to understand that God takes the business of the church very seriously.

Remember King Uzziah! He was a good king and did so many things to please the Lord, but then He began to swell with pride. He didn't think he needed the priests anymore. He could do everything by himself. So, he took a sensor filled with incense, set it on fire, and went into the temple to do what God had anointed the priests to do. He tried to take an anointing that was not his, and God brought his disobedient act to a sudden and complete stop. The priests tried to stop him and warned him of the danger of disobeying God in the matter of the holy things. But Uzziah raged against the priests and made threats toward them. Then, King Uzziah broke out in leprosy, and he was driven from the temple and from his own throne. The next thing we read about Uzziah is that he rested with his fathers. This is serious business. If you play with the fire of God, you can get burned. Don't ever try to step into another person's anointing or go outside what God has already anointed you to do. This is serious business.

A key element in warfare is something called "Command and Control." This is one of the most important elements in combat operations. Leaders must be able to communicate with subordinates in battle. Communication is essential, because when the bullets start flying, there will be times when no one is answering the phone. That's why they have the headsets built into their helmets today. Because when the bullets are flying you begin to think about one thing and one thing only: surviving. Instead of doing what you are supposed to do according to the battle plan, you begin to seek cover or take evasive actions. In wartime when bullets are flying and your mission is to assault that building, you don't want to do it, because your life is being threatened.

Command and control gives the leader the ability to continue to issue orders like, "Get up from there and go! Take that building, now!" Unless you respond together and follow commands, people are going to die, and others will be seriously wounded. Remember warfare in the natural and in the spiritual puts you into a life and death situation.

From our training and our experience we have come to know that command and control is critically important. In combat an army will absolutely collapse when the leadership loses command and control. We saw it in both wars in Iraq. When Saddam Hussein lost command and control and went into hiding in a small hole in the ground, his army fell apart.

You need to lock this concept into your minds and remain aware of it: When command and control is lost a military unit falls apart. So, if you plan to be God's Special Forces, you must have command and control working.

In time of war, one of the first things you want to do is knock out the enemy's command and control system before he can respond effectively.

The Spirit of Prophecy is God's command and control system. Remember the wonderful Biblical story of the prophet Elisha. Elisha was a very powerful man in his service to the Lord and in his anointing. God would tell Elisha the enemy's locations and movements before they actually happened. Then Elisha would go to the king of Israel and report it. He would say, "Now, don't go to that valley, there is an ambush there." The ambush would be foiled. He would say, "Don't go over by that stream today, they have set up an ambush." Elisha was regularly pointing out all of the enemy's weak spots.

After a period of time, the king of Aram got offended, because over and over his plans failed. You know how dictatorial types of leaders can act in times like this. He decided that he had a spy on his own staff. He thought, "Right here in my war room, I have spies, because someone is leaking information over to the king of Israel." So, he decided to locate him and kill him. He was about ready to line all of them up against a wall and execute them. He probably thought he would be better off starting over with some fresh leaders who were loyal. Then, one of his officers explained what was happening:

*"And the man of God sent to the king of Israel, saying, "Beware that you do not pass this place, for the Syrians are coming down there." Then the king of Israel sent someone to the place of which the man of God had told him. Thus he warned him, and he was watchful there, not just once or twice. Therefore the heart of the king of Syria was greatly troubled by this thing; and he called his servants and said to them, "Will you not show me which of us is for the king of Israel?" And one of his servants said, "None, my lord, O king; but Elisha, the prophet who is in Israel, tells the king of Israel the words that you speak in your bedroom." (2 Kings 6:9-12)*

God was speaking so specifically to Elisha that he knew the smallest details of the enemy's plan. Have you ever experienced that? In times of intense conflict in the church, God has shown me visions of rebellious people — I see exactly where they are standing in their homes, and I can hear their conversation. I have experienced that several times. Remember that the Holy Spirit is the Command and Control element of the Lord.

How would you like for someone to tell your enemies what you say in your bedroom? This was very disconcerting for the king, and he took quick action in an attempt to stop Elisha from serving the king of Israel in this manner. Basically he said, "let's take out their command and control element!" He tried to kill Elisha. In his mind this would take out God's command and control system. He didn't just send an assassin or a small raiding party. He took the entire army in order to fight against this one prophet.

If you have read this story you know the outcome. By himself (with God's help) the prophet Elisha took the whole army captive. Are you getting an idea of how powerful God intends this to be?

The Apostle Peter prophesied that this powerful Spirit was what came upon the 120 disciples gathered in the upper room on the Day of Pentecost. He proclaimed that this powerful Spirit of prophesy which came upon all them had been prophesied long ago by Joel. In Acts 2, we get a picture of Peter standing up and giving his first really good sermon. We see the entire group of disciples in unity for the first time. Peter stood up under the inspiration of the Holy Spirit and said:

*"But this is what was spoken by the prophet Joel: 'And it shall come to pass in the last days, says God, That I will pour out of My Spirit on all flesh; Your sons and your daughters shall prophesy, Your young men shall see visions, Your old men shall dream dreams. And on My menservants and on My maidservants I will pour*

*out My Spirit in those days; And they shall prophesy.'"*
(Acts 2:16-18)

Notice that this prophesy is given twice in scripture. First by Joel in chapter 2, verses 28-32 and again in Acts 2:16-21. When God tells you something twice (like this prophetic word) what does it mean? It means that it is established or decreed by the Lord, and it is certain.

When people observed what was happening on the day of Pentecost, what did they see? They saw a bunch of people acting like they were drunk early in the morning. And they heard people speaking in tongues. But, when Peter got up to speak, he didn't talk about being drunk in the Spirit. He didn't mention speaking in tongues. What did Peter talk about? He talked about prophecy, visions, and dreams. Because Peter saw by the inspiration of the Holy Spirit that something had arrived which the outsiders couldn't see. There was so much more happening than drunken behavior, speaking in tongues and winning people to Christ. Something important for God's people had changed! Something had shifted in the Spirit realm. However, this was only the beginning. It had not yet come to "all flesh."

And, I believe that even today, we have not experienced the fullness of that prophecy from Joel. I believe that today we are still waiting to see the fulfillment and completeness of the prophecy that Peter referenced on the day of Pentecost. And I believe that NOW is the time, as the bride is being prepared for Jesus' return and as the great wedding feast of the Lamb grows nearer. Many other people, well known and recognized for their prophetic gifting, are saying that a huge shift in the prophetic is about to take place. They are seeing and proclaiming that there will be a sudden powerful shift in the prophetic in the very near future.

I believe that what we are seeing now is God preparing to establish His end-time command and control system. He has always intended this prophetic outpouring to come into being in order to help prepare the Bride for Jesus' return. I believe that this is true. I believe we are in that time right now. There are so many signs, so many things happening as we see more and more people operating in the prophetic. Beyond just a few receiving a simple prophetic gifting, we are seeing large numbers of people emerging as prophets, and the things they are prophesying are coming true. Remember the Biblical test to confirm a prophet? Does what he or she says come true?

Many of these prophetic voices are proclaiming that you and I are about to see this huge shift which is coming. It will be a time when people will stop operating merely as individuals, and begin to work as a team. This is the time for a powerful army of the Lord to emerge. It is time for each of us to merge with the body and become a vital part of God's Special Forces. These Special Forces will become a prophetic army which will speak God's Word with such accuracy that people in the world are going to begin to wonder what is happening. They will want to know what kind of gifts are these people manifesting which allow them to say these things with such clarity and accuracy? And I believe that we are about to see that in our generation! Amen? Are you ready for it?

This is something we can all get excited about. And, I pray that we will all begin to feel a desire building from within to enlist in these Special Forces of God. But, before we do, I want you to know one very important thing.

## WHEN THE SPIRIT OF PROPHESY COMES THE ENEMY RESPONDS!

When the enemy sees this powerful Spirit coming into God's people and transforming them into a mighty army, the enemy will always respond in a powerful way. Look at Malachi 4:5: Now this passage and the verse after it contain the last words of the Old Testament. There is only one more verse after verse five. So, the next to the last verse of the Old Testament speaks of the coming millennial reign of Christ. God speaks a grand promise through the prophet Malachi.

*"Behold, I will send you Elijah the prophet Before the coming of the great and dreadful day of the Lord."* (Malachi 4:5)

All students of the New Testament know that John the Baptist came in the spirit of Elijah. We are literally (like the words of the song) living in the days of Elijah, because the spirit of Elijah is in us.

When this prophecy is fulfilled, it will be an unprecedented time of power in the spirit. This teaching and these promises are woven into the entire Bible. You may wonder as I did, "How could the church have missed it all this time?" And, yet we have missed it for so long.

James 5:17a (NIV) says, *"Elijah was a man just like us."* Did you get that? Elijah was just like you! You are the same as Elijah! Are you catching this? Then James gives us an example of what Elijah did in the second half of this verse, *"He prayed earnestly that it would not rain, and it did not rain on the land for three and a half years."* (James 5:17b, NIV) James, the brother of Jesus and head of the church in Jerusalem, wants you to know that you have that kind of prophetic power available to you. You have the prophetic power to pray and stop the rain for three and a half years. These truly are the days of Elijah... and...This kind of power will not go unnoticed by the enemy. The enemy always sends a spirit against the Spirit of prophecy, and it's always the same spirit.

Because the first person who really exhibited this spirit was so adept at it, the spirit has been named after her. It is the spirit of Jezebel. And, I want you to know that the Jezebel spirit does not want to be talked about. Jezebel does not like to be preached about. Jezebel will come against anyone who operates in the prophetic. Jezebel will come after any pastor who preaches about her, because she does not want you to know about her or how she operates.

The enemy has used this spirit of Jezebel so effectively for so long, that he wants us to be unaware of its existence and how it operates. So, the enemy comes strongly against anyone who teaches or studies this. But, if you are living in obedience to the Lord and operating in the prophetic, I want you to know that the spirit of Jezebel is coming against you whether you speak about her or not.

Elijah was a powerful man of God who was fearless and strong. We read about his courageous actions in 1 Kings and in James. He was a powerful man who stood up to many powerful people. On one occasion, he stood up to King Ahab, 450 prophets of Baal, 400 prophets of Asherah, and all of their worshippers in Israel. This happened on Mount Carmel and with God's help, he destroyed them. After defeating them in the battle over sacrificial fire, he killed all of the false prophets with a sword. In this incident he was fearless. He stood before all these people without a hint of fear. But, when Jezebel came against him, what happened? When Jezebel said she would kill him, he ran for his life. He stood up without fear against hundreds and against thousands. But the moment this one woman, Jezebel, came against him, he ran in fear. In this account, you see that Jezebel was the real power in Israel. Ahab was weak, whiny, and easily manipulated. He was morally bankrupt and had no power in the spirit. Jezebel was a powerful manipulator who was accustomed to getting her way. She controlled Ahab like a puppet on a string. Notice what the Bible says about Ahab and Jezebel:

*"There was never a man like Ahab, who sold himself to do evil in the eyes of the LORD, urged on by Jezebel his wife."* (1 Kings 21:25, NIV)

Jezebel was not the king, but she controlled him in everything he attempted to do. In her behavior, we see that a Jezebel spirit will stop at nothing to get her way. She doesn't care who she hurts, and she will attempt to destroy anyone who gets in her way. She is not concerned about anyone else's feelings. And when it is all over, she will feel good about what she has done to get her way.

Jezebel hates prophecy, wisdom, revelation, counsel, and the anointing. She will come against the prophetic with a vicious display of power which often leaves the entire church immobilized in shock and fear. You need to know that she will come against anyone operating in the prophetic. When you begin to flow in the prophetic gifts or receive a mantle as a prophet, you will have to do battle with the Jezebel spirit whether you want to or not.

One of the ways you can recognize a Jezebel spirit is that she will come against pastors. The Jezebel spirit has been doing this for generation after generation. At the writing of this book, I have been in the ministry for over 43 years, and I have met Jezebel many times in those years. I can tell you from experience that Jezebel is a powerful spirit. And, when you don't know what is happening; when you don't understand it, it is so easy to just give in. If you are not aware and prepared when she comes, you will get lost in the fog of war, because you just don't have time to analyze it and get a handle on it. You will be like Elijah and just shift into a survival mode.

If you are operating in the prophetic, she will come against you. If you are a pastor, especially a pastor with a prophetic gifting, she will come against you. If you are called into any form of ministry, she will come against you. In other words, you cannot avoid this spirit. It is not a matter of "if" but of "when" she will come against you. I will not pull any punches. I want you to know that she is powerful, and she is deadly. She will stop at nothing! And, she doesn't just want to control one person. Jezebel wants to control everyone, and she will not rest until she is in complete control.

[NOTE: We have been using the term she because the first person to demonstrate this spirit so effectively happened to be a woman. But, be aware that men can also have a Jezebel spirit. The spirit is not gender specific. I am using the word "she" because Jezebel was a woman. Someone said that "Jezebel was so bad that they retired her name." You don't find very many kids who have been named Jezebel. This is important to note because when the Jezebel spirit shows up again in the seven churches in the Revelation of John, it is not because a person actually had the name. It is about a spiritual force at work in one or more people.]

We must come to accept the fact that the Jezebel spirit will not rest until she has absolute control over everyone in her area. But the good news is that these enemy spirits are not very creative. They use the same methods over and over again. They don't really have to change because we allow ourselves to be fooled over and over the same way. As a result, we will always see a Jezebel spirit using one or more of her three primary tactics:

1) She will first try to manipulate people, situations, or resources to get her way.
2) If this fails, she moves to abusive power to try control others.
3) If necessary, she resorts to fear tactics to manipulate and control.

Over the centuries, this spirit has been successful at destroying families, friendships, businesses, and churches. She causes so much turmoil and pain that finally people will seek peace at any cost. People will finally say, "Okay! Whatever you say! Whatever you want! Just give us peace! We can't take any more of this!" But as long as Jezebel is around there will be no peace. She will not stop. Don't be fooled by a temporary period of peace. She is just building up for another major attack.

She uses moods, pouting, the silent treatment, and any other tactic you can think up to gain and retain control. She will use any or all of these tactics to get her way. She is not ashamed of it. It doesn't embarrass her. She will do it consistently until everyone says, "Okay, Okay, we will do it your way." One of her favorite tricks is to use money to manipulate the church. She will suggest that she may withhold her tithes and offerings or her building fund pledge if she doesn't get her way. Many churches are so dependent on the weekly offerings to pay large mortgages and program costs that they will just give in to protect their income. Jesus warned that we can't serve both God and money. But, many churches try to do just that.

This gives you a very clear and unique picture of the Jezebel spirit. There's not just one spirit running around causing trouble. If that were true, you could gather around her, bind her up, and send her back to the pit. However, the enemy works through demonic oppression to work this spirit in groups. This happens in businesses, families, churches, and social groups. I have watched the Jezebel spirit jump from person to person in a meeting making it almost impossible to pin her down. And, that is why we have to fight her in groups. You must stand behind your pastor or leader to deal with this spirit.

*"And it came to pass after these things that Naboth the Jezreelite had a vineyard which was in Jezreel, next to the palace of Ahab king of Samaria. So Ahab spoke to Naboth, saying, "Give me your vineyard, that I may have it for a vegetable garden, because it is near, next to my house; and for it I will give you a vineyard better than it. Or, if it seems good to you, I will give you its worth in money." But Naboth said to Ahab, "The Lord*

*forbid that I should give the inheritance of my fathers to you!"* (1 Kings 21:1-3)

To really understand this, you must have an understanding of the law in Israel at that time. Remember that every 50 years there was a year of Jubilee. That year all family property went back to the original family; even if it had been sold or traded. But, if you sold it to a king, it was gone forever. However, the garden the king gives to you will go back to the original family in the year of Jubilee, and your family will have no inheritance. So you must understand that Naboth was not just being arbitrary. He was trying to protect his family's inheritance.

*"So Ahab went into his house sullen and displeased because of the word which Naboth the Jezreelite had spoken to him; for he had said, "I will not give you the inheritance of my fathers." And he lay down on his bed, and turned away his face, and would eat no food. But Jezebel his wife came to him, and said to him, "Why is your spirit so sullen that you eat no food?" He said to her, "Because I spoke to Naboth the Jezreelite, and said to him, 'Give me your vineyard for money; or else, if it pleases you, I will give you another vineyard for it.' And he answered, 'I will not give you my vineyard.'" Then Jezebel his wife said to him, "You now exercise authority over Israel! Arise, eat food, and let your heart be cheerful; I will give you the vineyard of Naboth the Jezreelite."* (1 Kings 21:4-7)

Jezebel was saying in effect; "You want to see some power. I'll show you some power! I can make this thing work out. Watch how it's done." So, in this passage you can see the character of Ahab, and you can see the character of Jezebel. Here we see the strength of the Jezebel spirit beginning to emerge. Look closely at how she opeates. She uses other people to get her way. She uses other people to do her dirty work. She uses the eunuchs in the palace, influential people, and scoundrels to accomplish her purpose. She uses the leaders, deacons, and elders to do her dirty work and help her get her way. If anyone catches her, she has plausible deniability. She will place the blame on whoever helped her.

> *"So the men of his city, the elders and nobles who were inhabitants of his city, did as Jezebel had sent to them, as it was written in the letters which she had sent to them. They proclaimed a fast, and seated Naboth with high honor among the people. And two men, scoundrels, came in and sat before him; and the scoundrels witnessed against him, against Naboth, in the presence of the people, saying, "Naboth has blasphemed God and the king!" Then they took him outside the city and stoned him with stones, so that he died. Then they sent to Jezebel, saying, "Naboth has been stoned and is dead." And it came to pass, when Jezebel heard that Naboth had been stoned and was dead, that Jezebel said to Ahab, "Arise, take possession of the vineyard of Naboth the Jezreelite, which he refused to give you for money; for Naboth is not alive, but dead." So it was, when Ahab heard that Naboth was dead, that Ahab got up and went down to take possession of the vineyard of Naboth the Jezreelite."* (1 Kings 21:11-16)

Jezebel has no remorse. She can come against you and kill you or destroy your reputation and not have even one bit of compassion. She will not even show a hint of empathy for you. She will lie about you. She will bring others to lie about you, and ruin you in the community, and feel absolutely no remorse. The only thing that matters to a Jezebel spirit is getting their way; getting what they want.

Jezebel hates the 5-fold offices of ministry: and she especially hates the office of the prophet. God uses the prophet to expose evil. So, the prophet will expose a Jezebel spirit. Do you desire the gift of prophecy? Do you want to have a strong anointing in the prophetic? Know this: the Jezebel spirit will come against you! The stronger your prophetic anointing, the stronger she will come against you. So be prepared. She is powerful and she will come against you. And, she can cause so much intimidation that the prophet will begin to wonder if he/she is anointed at all. Some people under attack by a Jezebel spirit have questioned whether God has even spoken to them. They begin to wonder if they are doing anything right. You see, you can wind up like Elijah running in fear in order to get away from her threats.

I want to give you a diagnostic tool you can use to identify this spirit in churches. The spirit of Jezebel will always try to destroy the influence of the pastor's wife. If someone comes to you criticizing the pastor's wife, be on guard, you are probably face to face with the Jezebel spirit. She will try to discredit the pastor's wife to the point that she will want to leave the church or even the marriage to get some relief. At times this spirit has been known to pray publicly for the pastor's wife to be removed. In extreme cases, she has prayed for the pastor's wife to be removed through a divorce or even for her to physically die. This is a very nasty spirit and she will actually pray against the pastor's wife.

**A STRONG WARNING**: You should never pray against people! You pray to God; you lift up the situation; and you pray for His will to be done. But, you don't pray against people. Our battle is not against flesh and blood.

But this shameless spirit of Jezebel will pray against people; especially she will come against the prophet, the pastor, and the pastor's wife. She wants to control the church and the pastor, and she tries to eliminate anyone else who can influence him/her.

She will bring all kinds of criticisms and judgments against the pastor's wife to the pastor hoping to drive a wedge between them. I know this because it has happened to me. When it happens, you look at someone and wonder, "Who do you think you are that I would choose you over my wife? You must be insane!" Here is the diagnostic key again: if you're ever in a church and someone comes out to destroy the credibility of the pastor's wife: Who are you seeing? It is most certainly the Jezebel spirit.

This brings us to a really big question:

## HOW DO YOU DEAL WITH THE SPIRIT OF JEZEBEL?

First: you must examine yourself and ensure that you are 100% free from the influence of the Jezebel spirit. Apply all the tests to yourself.

1. Are you speaking out against or openly opposing the prophetic gifting in others?

2. Are you being openly critical or judgmental toward the five-fold office of ministry in your church or group?

3. Are you attacking the pastor's wife and trying to marginalize her to reduce her influence?

4. Are you insisting on getting your way at all costs?

5. Are you determined to control people to get the outcomes you desire?

6. Are you unconcerned when others get hurt or injured by your attacks?

If you find that the Jezebel spirit is manifesting through you, do everything possible to cast that spirit out, and if necessary seek help from a deliverance ministry. Place a claim on Jesus' promise in Luke 10:18-19, "And He said to them, "I saw Satan fall like lightning from heaven. Behold, I give you the authority to trample on serpents and scorpions, and over all the power of the enemy, and nothing shall by any means hurt you."

Remember God's commandment found in 1 Chronicles 16:22 and Psalm 105:15, *"Do not touch My anointed ones, and do My prophets no harm."* When God says something twice, it is established (see Genesis 41:32, "And the dream was repeated to Pharaoh twice because the thing *is* established by God, and God will shortly bring it to pass.") If you are attacking or being judgmental toward those anointed for ministry or attempting to bring harm to a prophet or someone with a prophetic anointing, you may be under the influence of a Jezebel spirit. Break it off quickly before you can do more harm.

Second: Remember what Moses did when he was confronted: he fell on his face before God, and let God deal with it. When Leviathan comes, you fall face down and let God deal with it. But, what do you do with a Jezebel spirit? The scriptures make us aware that there are some things which God expects us to do ourselves.

*"Now when Jehu had come to Jezreel, Jezebel heard of it; and she put paint on her eyes and adorned her head, and looked through a window. Then, as Jehu entered at the gate, she said, "Is it peace, Zimri, murderer of your master?" And he looked up at the window, and said, "Who is on my side? Who?" So two or three eunuchs looked out at him. Then he said, "Throw her down."*

*So they threw her down, and some of her blood spattered on the wall and on the horses; and he trampled her underfoot."* (2 Kings 9:30-33)

The very people she had been using to do her dirty work were the ones called on to cast her out or throw her down. Remember we are talking about the spirit and not the person. We do not war against flesh and blood, but against demonic forces. We cannot accommodate them, tolerate them, or compromise with them. They have to go. Jezebel was so given over to that spirit that she had to die for the spirit to be cast out. The end of her life was terrible. Jezebel didn't even get a funeral. When they came back to get her, the dogs had taken her away, just as prophesied.

The only way to deal with a Jezebel spirit, is to cast it out. The person oppressed by this spirit cannot stop on her/his own. She must be delivered. She will not stop until the church casts her out. This is the only way to deal with it, but always remember, you cast out the spirit and not the person. I am repeating some things because you must learn them so well that they become a part of you and the way you minister. So, remember that your battle is not against flesh and blood, and you don't want to start capriciously throwing people out of the church. However, if the person refuses to change, then the person has to go, but do it with love leaving open the possibility of restoration and return.

In dealing with a Jezebel spirit, it is essential for the congregation to support the pastor. He can't do it alone. Jezebel causes so much trouble that weaker people will give in. They will choose to make peace by tolerating her behavior. But, remember what Jesus said to the church of Thyatira (see Revelation 2:18-29) about tolerating this spirit.

Some people will want to keep Jezebel, because they want to keep her tithe or get her pledge for a building project. Jezebel loves to use money as a means of control. She withholds her giving until she gets what she wants. When this happens a church is in trouble because she has already created a dependence on her and her money which makes it extremely difficult for most congregations to break free. To keep things running smoothly, they want to make peace, but there will be no peace as long as she is around. If you decide to tolerate her, she will keep on attacking, until finally people are simply worn out and give in. When this happens, in the name of securing peace, they will back off and let her have her way.

Over and over, I have seen and experienced people leaving the pastor standing alone with egg on his face. He has attempted to get the group to cast her out, but they back away and let him suffer the consequences. They may even ask the pastor to leave the church thinking that will bring peace. But, as long as the Jezebel spirit is there, there will be no peace. She will simply wait for the next pastor and then go through the same painful process to achieve control or eliminate the new leader if she can't get it.

I cannot emphasize enough the need for us to stand together in unity of spirit and purpose to eliminate this threat to the church. We will never reach our full potential until she is gone. The Jezebel spirit must not have control!

## JEZEBEL MUST NOT BE ALLOWED TO BE IN CONTROL!

This is why the Jezebel spirit doesn't want us to talk about her. She likes to work behind the scenes. You know people like that! In business, they're behind the scenes controlling things. They are especially pleased to have control over the money because often the power is with the money. And this spirit will use weak people to accomplish her purpose. When things explode, the person in the public eye usually gets blamed and receives all the criticism, while Jezebel remains hidden and safe. So the Jezebel spirit likes to work behind the scenes where she can continue to make herself look good. In these situations the people in official positions are just as helpless and hopeless as anyone else.

But if we want to do what God wants us to do — if we want to operate in God's way, we have got to deal with her, but it has to be done together and in unity of purpose. And, it is important to know that we are all vulnerable to this spirit. Any one of us can begin to exhibit a Jezebel spirit if we don't stay in God's purpose. We need to stay open to the prophetic for God to reveal to us what is going on inside our own lives, families, and churches.

I want to give you some strong advice (especially to the men). In the military you learn that to be an effective leader you must not humiliate people in public. Everyone loses confidence in a leader who dresses people down in front of their peers. They immediately think, "I could be next." If you lose the trust of your people, you become ineffective in your leadership position.

The Jezebel spirit works in men to embarrass and humiliate their wives and children publically. You never look good or strong doing this. People will see the spirit working in you and lose respect for you. Ironically, most people resort to publicly attacking their own family in an attempt to make themselves look good. They are willing to make family members look bad in order to accomplish their goal. But it always produces the opposite result. So men, you must stay away from this behavior, because it weakens your influence with everyone.

The Jezebel spirit works in women to embarrass and humiliate their husbands publically in order to get their way, but it never works out the way you might hope. If you make your spouse look bad to others, it calls your judgment into question. How could you have had the poor judgment to select such a person for a mate and why have you stayed with him? The Jezebel spirit never gives you what you seek most. Because she comes from the enemy, and her spirit is identical to his.

She wants to use you to hurt others and then turn on you to steal your blessing, kill your effectiveness in the kingdom, and destroy your work for the Lord. You must get free from this spirit to enjoy the fullness of the blessing.

The Jezebel spirit works in children to humiliate and embarrass their parents publically to get their way, but it backfires in so many ways. Young people, you may get what you want in the public setting, but the time is coming when you get home and experience the payback. You wind up blocking the flow of your own blessings and lose favor with the people who are most important in your life. The enemy has been so successful in driving wedges into families to separate them and bring pain and suffering in place of the promised joy of the Lord. Don't do it! The price is too high.

The Jezebel spirit in a church will try to embarrass, humiliate and marginalize the influence of all who are operating in the five-fold ministry anointing. She will focus especially on the prophet and the pastor in order to take all of the control and influence for herself. With an increase in the gift of discernment, you will be enabled to see more and more clearly that the Jezebel spirit is at work in people who demand their way in church. You would think that it would be embarrassing to do this in public. But, remember, the Jezebel spirit knows no shame and feels no remorse. This spirit is so destructive and so dangerous that for the church to fulfill her calling, you must learn to recognize these enemy attacks and deal with them quickly. If you don't, she will take you right out of the game. She completely incapacitated Elijah, and he ran for his life.

*"Suddenly a voice came to him, and said, "What are you doing here, Elijah?" And he said, "I have been very zealous for the Lord God of hosts; because the children of Israel have forsaken Your covenant, torn down Your altars, and killed Your prophets with the sword. I*

*alone am left; and they seek to take my life."* (1 Kings 19:13b-14)

God showed Elijah His power and His glory, and asked him again what he was doing there. Elijah gave the same answer over and over. He was broken, and could not recover. God saw it in each of his answers. Elijah simply could not get past this defeat. He could not be restored. And since he couldn't recover, God took him out of the game and replaced him with Elisha.

*"The Lord said to him, "Go back the way you came, and go to the Desert of Damascus. When you get there, anoint Hazael king over Aram. Also, anoint Jehu son of Nimshi king over Israel, and anoint Elisha son of Shaphat from Abel Meholah to succeed you as prophet. Jehu will put to death any who escape the sword of Hazael, and Elisha will put to death any who escape the sword of Jehu. Yet I reserve seven thousand in Israel— all whose knees have not bowed down to Baal and all whose mouths have not kissed him."* (1 Kings 19:15-18, NIV)

This did not mean that Elijah was lost or going to hell. It didn't mean that God didn't love him anymore. God made that very clear to us. Remember, God promised that Elijah would come back to usher in the era of the Messiah. Elijah was on the Mount of Transfiguration with Jesus, and brought encouragement from the Father as He prepared for His sacrifice on the cross. Restored in heaven, Elijah comes back in power to bless and support Jesus. If you ever think that God rejected Elijah, just look at the last promise made by the Lord in the Old Testament.

*"Behold, I will send you Elijah the prophet before the coming of the great and dreadful day of the Lord. And*

*he will turn the hearts of the fathers to the children, and
the hearts of the children to their fathers, lest I come
and strike the earth with a curse."* (Malachi 4:5-6)

This story of Elijah gives a clear picture to us today about
dealing with Jezebel. If you let her break you or cause you
to run in fear, God will work to restore you. But, if you can't
make a comeback — if you just can't recover, God will replace
you. God's work must be done; if not by you, then by your
replacement. Jezebel's intent is that she will take you out or
that she will make you so weak that God will take you out.
That's Jezebel. She's powerful, and we have to deal with her
together if we are going to stand.

## TO PLEASE GOD, IN THESE LAST DAYS, WE MUST OPERATE IN THE SPIRIT OF PROPHECY

We must do it even though we know that Jezebel will come
for us. We have to operate in the prophetic in order to be God's
command and control system. We must deal with her in order
to fight the good fight and become more than conquerors in this
spiritual warfare. The initial and key concept is that Jezebel is
not gone. Remember Jesus' letter to Thyatira. It is unlikely that
any woman there was actually named Jezebel, but there was a
woman in that congregation that was controlled by the Jezebel
spirit.

*"Nevertheless, I have this against you: You tolerate that
woman Jezebel, who calls herself a prophetess. By her
teaching she misleads my servants into sexual immorality and the eating of food sacrificed to idols. I have
given her time to repent of her immorality, but she is
unwilling. So I will cast her on a bed of suffering, and
I will make those who commit adultery with her suffer
intensely, unless they repent of her ways. I will strike*

*her children dead (that's what Jehu did — he killed all of the house of Ahab). Then all the churches will know that I am he who searches hearts and minds, and I will repay each of you according to your deeds. Now I say to the rest of you in Thyatira, to you who do not hold to her teaching and have not learned Satan's so-called deep secrets (I will not impose any other burden on you): Only hold on to what you have until I come. To him who overcomes and does my will to the end, I will give authority over the nations..."* (Revelation 2:20-26, NIV)

I want to tell you that if you think you are going to operate in the power of the Holy Spirit; if you think you are going to take it to the nations; and if you think you are going to be a kingdom carrier, but you tolerate a Jezebel spirit and allow her to operate in your church, you're just kidding yourself. It will not happen.

## JESUS' MESSAGE IS FOR NOW

This message from Jesus is for NOW! It's for the church age. Remember: Malachi 4:5, *"See, I will send you the prophet Elijah before that great and dreadful day of the LORD comes."* Know this for certain: If we are living in the days of Elijah, we're also living in the days of Jezebel. If we don't deal with the spirit of Jezebel, we will face judgment from our Lord Jesus

If you want authority over the nations, you must begin by dealing with Jezebel. God will not bless a ministry that lets Jezebel corrupt the church. God will not bless a prophet who cowers and runs from Jezebel. God won't bless a church which tolerates a Jezebel spirit.

The pastor must have the support of the people to oust Jezebel. This rarely happens in churches today. We are living

67

in the days of inclusiveness and political correctness, and Jezebel has learned how to use that against us. We can end up feeling compelled to make everyone happy and to accommodate everyone. We live in a day when "Peace at all costs" rules over most of the churches. So, Jezebel has had a free reign for hundreds of years. This has happened primarily because the people will not stand with the pastor against this spirit.

She is very strong and we can only deal with her if we do it together. When we stand together, God will send the spirit of prophecy. God will give us the Spirit of wisdom and understanding, counsel and might, and knowledge and the fear of the Lord. He will give us all we need to handle it, but we have got to handle it. If you want the nations; if you want to do what God wants you to do, you must oust the Jezebel spirit. This is one of the main purposes for the spirit of prophesy — to kick Jezebel out.

The Spirit of prophecy comes to establish God's end-time army's command and control system. And Jezebel's purpose is to hinder it and if possible block it all together. Remember, when you go into battle, one of the first things you want to do is to take out the enemy's command and control system.

An illustration from Desert Storm: The day before the invasion of Iraq was to take place, the helicopters of the 101$^{st}$ Airborne Division, the Screaming Eagles, went in at night and took out the radar sites and the command and control communication towers in the region. The next morning as they were flying back from their missions, the fighter jets and bombers flew over them unhampered by enemy radar. The enemy leaders had lost the ability to communicate with their troops. Chaplain Herb Kitchens wrote a song about that mission called, "The Night the Eagle Screamed"

That is what Jezebel wants to do to the body of Christ. She wants to take out God's end-times command and control system. You must stop her and cast her out, and remove the enemy's command and control system at the same time. And, you need to do it now.

Again, I caution you to be aware that if you are operating in the prophetic, you can't avoid it, Jezebel is going to come against you. Where do you stand? What are you going to do? It is time for us to seize the initiative; take the battle to the enemy; and bring shock and awe as we cast out the spirit of Jezebel.

*prayer*

## PRAYER FOR GOD'S HELP

Father God, we pray that you would help us to have eyes to see and ears to hear. Lord, may we know when we are up against Jezebel. May we see the tactics and know what to do. May we learn, Lord, to stand together. May we reach out and join together, arm in arm, as a fire and maneuver team to accomplish your purpose for our church and our ministry. Lord, we ask today that you would release a new level in the prophetic; a fresh anointing in the gifts of the Spirit, that we could be an effective part of your Special Forces.

Lord, give us boldness to stand — the courage to stand against this wicked spirit, Jezebel. Lord help us we pray, and Lord may we never displease you by tolerating evil in our midst. Lord, on the day of judgment, we want to hear you say, "Hey, hey, hey! Well done! You did a good job! I'm proud of you son! I'm proud of you daughter! Lord, we don't want to hear, "Uh Oh! I never knew you!" Lord God we want to please you! Help us. We need boldness! We need strength! We need the prophetic. Lord, release your command and control element into this Special Forces Unit in your church. We ask it together in the glorious name of Yeshua ha Messiach! Amen and Amen!

# LESSON 2

# "THE SPIRIT OF TRUTH"

This is the second training session of spiritual boot-camp! You've been learning some basic skills for spiritual warfare. One of these skills is to learn how to get an understanding of the enemy's intent and capabilities. Remember what Jesus said about this in Luke 14.

> *"Or suppose a king is about to go to war against another king. Will he not first sit down and consider whether he is able with ten thousand men to oppose the one coming against him with twenty thousand? If he is not able, he will send a delegation while the other is still a long way off and will ask for terms of peace."* (Luke 14:31-32, NIV)

By way of a short review, what do you need to know about your ancient enemy, the devil? First, you need to know what the enemy intends to do, how he operates, what resources and capabilities he has. Then, you need to know his objective: Jesus helped us with that in John, chapter 10:

*"The thief does not come except to steal, and to kill, and to destroy. I have come that they may have life, and that they may have it more abundantly."* (John 10:10)

In addition to knowing the enemy's intent, you need to know about the weapons of your warfare. I watched an episode of the TV show "PSYCH," in which the lead character, Sean, was trying to show how cool he was in a military armory, As he picked up a weapon and held it in front of himself, he asked the expert what it was and the expert replied, "It is a LAW, a light anti-tank weapon, and you are pointing it at yourself."

Out of ignorance, we have too often picked up the enemy's weapons and pointed them at ourselves. We must become familiar with his primary weapons. He consistently uses confusion, deception, and falsehood. We know that his methods are designed to hinder our relationships with God, and prevent us from reaching our God given destiny. He wants to prevent us from accomplishing God's purpose for our lives, and he has designed his weapons to tempt us to turn against each other. When the enemy gets into our camp and we turn to fire on him, what happens? We begin to shoot one another. We saw that clearly happening in the previous lesson. The Jezebel spirit comes in through someone in the group and begins to attack from within. When we try to deal with her, we often wind up hurting each other. If this is allowed to go on indefinitely, everyone is likely to end up getting wounded in the battle.

Remember when God told Moses to send spies in to the promised land to check it out before they entered to take possession of it. The spies were given very specific things to look for. If you were to look at the current military doctrine on what you are to look for when you go into an area to gather intelligence on the enemy, you would find that Moses basically used the same concepts in his instructions to the spies. The leadership got it right, but ten of the spies completely missed the point.

They made two tragic tactical errors in their calculations. First, they overestimate the enemy's strength and capabilities.

> *"But the men who had gone up with him said, "We are not able to go up against the people, for they are stronger than we." And they gave the children of Israel a bad report of the land which they had spied out, saying, "The land through which we have gone as spies is a land that devours its inhabitants, and all the people whom we saw in it are men of great stature. There we saw the giants (the descendants of Anak came from the giants); and we were like grasshoppers in our own sight, and so we were in their sight."* (Numbers 13:31-33)

Overestimating the enemy is a serious mistake which can lead to making some very bad decisions about the upcoming operations. When you overestimate the enemy, you instill fear and dread among your own forces. You are defeating your-self in the psychological warfare which always precedes a big battle.

The second and more critical mistake they made was to underestimate their friendly forces. This happened because in their estimate of friendly forces, they did not factor in God. After they had crossed the Red Sea with pharaoh's army in hot pursuit and God spoke to them through Moses saying, "The Egyptians you see today, you will never see again;" and after God destroyed the entire Egyptian Army before their eyes without them lifting a finger, they came back from their trip into the land stating that they were not capable of winning. They came to this conclusion because they did not factor God into the estimate. If you are serving God and following His guidance, you must always factor God and His power into your estimate of the situation. When we only look at the enemy's capability, we may lose heart like the children of Israel on that fateful day. The spies in Moses' day and people today make similar mistakes.

In any conflict, it is important to make a thorough estimate of your friendly forces. You need to know who is on your side. The US military has learned in the last 25-30 years how important it is to have a coalition of forces. Even if you are a large nation with powerful resources, it is a mistake to go into battle by yourself. But, if you can ally yourself with a number of other nations, then together you multiply your combat power and expand your range of capabilities.

When you make your estimate of friendly forces, you need to take into consideration all those people of God around you and the intercessors who are behind you. This is good, but it doesn't go far enough. You must also factor God into all your battle plans.

*"And I looked, and behold, in the midst of the throne and of the four living creatures, and in the midst of the elders, stood a Lamb as though it had been slain, having seven horns and seven eyes, which are the seven Spirits of God sent out into all the earth."* (Revelation 5:6)

This passage from John's Revelation is the primary scriptural passage for this training. In it you see that the seven Spirits have been sent out to be your allies: to war with you and to war for you. You must realize that you have not been left defenseless, and you have not been left without weapons of warfare. God has provided everything you need — NOW you need to train on the weapons of your warfare. If you have a powerful weapon and don't know how to use it, it is useless to you.

When I was stationed at Fort Campbell, Kentucky, I had to drive many military vehicles to accomplish all my assigned missions. I had to get a military drivers license in addition to my regular state drivers license in order to check vehicles out of the motor pool and use them. When I went to the driver's testing facility, I met some young soldiers and spent some time visiting with them. We were laughing and joking, and I was blessing them in the name of God. Eventually, I took my driving test, and afterward they handed me my new license. When I looked at the license, I was amazed to find out that I had been licensed not only to drive a sedan, a truck, and a jeep as I had requested, but I had also been licensed to drive all of the tactical vehicles in the entire division. Every vehicle the army owned had been checked off on my license. These young soldiers thought, "Well we'll help the chaplain. We will just authorize him to drive everything we have." And, that was what they did.

At that time, the army had a huge monstrous looking all-terrain vehicle called a "gamma goat." It had controls and mechanisms that were just weird to me, and I had no idea what purpose they served. During the next field training exercise, I was with a little band of soldiers who had gotten separated from our unit. To rejoin our unit, we had a long walk ahead of us. About half-way on our journey, we came upon one of the gamma-goats left there by some unit. When we saw this vehicle, we thought our problem was solved. The soldiers began to ask, "Is anyone licensed to drive this thing?" And, I said, "Well, yes! I am, but I don't even have a clue about how to start it. In fact, I don't even know how to get into it, much less drive it." We shrugged our soldiers and walked on toward our destination. The solution to the problem was at hand, but none of us knew how to make it work. The gamma goat was as useless to us as the tree it had been parked under by some unknown operator.

You may experience the same thing in your spiritual warfare. You may have a powerful vehicle or weapon at your disposal, but if you don't know how to use it, it is useless to you. In earthly warfare, you must know how to use your weapons and equipment. The same is true in spiritual warfare. Our weapons of spiritual warfare are mighty, and are able to bring down enemy strongholds. However, the question remains: "Are you qualified to use them?"

So far, we've studied one of these powerful weapons of spiritual warfare. These powerful weapons are the seven Spirits of God. We looked in some detail at the Spirit of Wisdom and Revelation (prophesy). What does the enemy send against this Spirit of God? He sends the spirit of Jezebel.

In this lesson we are going to look in some detail at another one of the seven Spirits of God. And, then we will become familiar with the spirit the enemy sends against it. Remember that the enemy sends his spirits in an attempt to block the flow of the Spirits of God in our lives and ministry.

Before Jesus ascended, He made a beautiful promise:

*"And I will ask the Father, and he will give you another Counselor to be with you forever—the Spirit of truth. The world cannot accept him, because it neither sees him nor knows him. But you know him, for he lives with you and will be in you."* (John 14:16-17, NIV)

How long did Jesus say that you get to have this Spirit with you? This spirit will be with you forever. Amen?

In this lesson, you will study in depth about the Spirit of truth. This is a very powerful Spirit which we desperately need in our battle against the devil. The heart of the real struggle in our spiritual warfare has always been between truth and falsehood.

## IT IS CRITICALLY IMPORTANT FOR US TO KNOW THE TRUTH.

There is so much deception in the world. Everywhere you look and everywhere you turn today you encounter deception. If you read the newspaper, listen to news programs, or watch TV, you will hear a great deal of deception. It has been said that if you listen to a lie long enough you will begin to believe it. Therefore, we desperately need to know the truth!

> *"We are from God, and whoever knows God listens to us; but whoever is not from God does not listen to us. This is how we recognize the Spirit of truth and the spirit of falsehood."* (1 John 4:6, NIV)

According to this passage of scripture, who does the enemy send against the Spirit of truth? Every time the Spirit of truth begins to work in our lives, the spirit of falsehood is close by. John makes the players in this battle perfectly clear.

There is a commercial for inclusiveness on American TV. This sleek advertisement is not for a product or service, but for an idea. It has several popular actors appealing for religious inclusiveness and sensitivity. One actor says, "I am a Christian." Another actor says, "I am a Jew." Another says, "I am spiritual." You know that this is gradually progressing to make a point. Finally, one actress says, "I believe in all paths to God" While this all seems nice and sweet, you must ask what is behind such an elaborate campaign to promote a world view approving everything.

The intense pressure to win a following for political correctness and religious inclusiveness may be the greatest deception in the world today. It is the belief that any old religion will get you there. After all, they are pretty much all the same. Right? Wrong! As you watch more and more of this deception of inclusiveness covering our world, you find that their message is not entirely true. Ask for the Holy Spirit to guide you into all truth, and He will reveal to you the purpose behind this ruse. According to the belief system behind this ad, there is a religion that is not generally accepted. This religion has been marginalized and demonized by the media and political leaders of our day. Do you know which religion this is? It is Christianity. The purpose of the movement for inclusiveness is designed to counter another world view; the world view of Christians who believe that Jesus is the only way to the Father. This very peaceful view is called hate. While a religion which demands submission, and calls for the death of all who refuse to submit is called peace by the same people. To buy into this world view requires you to be in deep deception, and it is being promoted in such subtle and seemingly harmless ways. This is the work of the spirit of falsehood.

If you enlist the help of the Spirit of truth and follow the progression of logic in this so called life philosophy of inclusiveness and political correctness, you will find that its proponents do not value or accept Christianity at all. The most vocal advocates of "inclusiveness" have continuously insinuated against and marginalized Christianity to make it the villain of the modern world. Many even refer to it as a religion of hate, and some are trying to make the basic beliefs of the faith hate crimes. All of this in spite of the fact that the true message of our faith is love, peace, and grace.

Unfortunately many among us have not helped to correct this mistaken image. Some in our groups have appeared in public to be so judgmental, so critical, so condemning, and so intolerant that the label "hater" seems to justly fit. The proponents of inclusiveness exempt this one group from the rules which they claim are being taught to prevent generalizations leading to prejudice. They maintain that hating and marginalizing Christianity is the right thing to do. We must avoid helping them to justify this belief. We are best at this when we live in love and bless others rather than cursing them. Jesus didn't do any of these hateful things. Jesus came with love and forgiveness. He embraced people and loved them into the kingdom. We need to work to change the false image of our faith. As the Bible says, "They will know us by the love we have for one another." But right now, this is just not part of the rules of political correctness.

At this point, I want you to understand another idea which is not deemed politically correct today. You must understand that without being a disciple, people can't really know the truth. You simply cannot know the truth if you are not a spirit-led disciple of Jesus Christ. This message is not about hate or exclusion. It is about helping other people, in a very loving way, to know the truth. Everyone is welcome to become a disciple of Jesus Christ, and have a loving relationship with the Father.

*"To the Jews who had believed him, Jesus said, "If you hold to my teaching, you are really my disciples. Then you will know the truth, and the truth will set you free."* (John 8:31-32, NIV)

Everyone likes that part about knowing the truth and being set free by the truth, but many are not too excited about verse 31. Verse 31 says you can't be a disciple unless you hold to the teachings of Jesus. You can't hold to the teachings of Jesus if you don't know them. So, amidst all this deception, how can we learn the truth correctly? God knew this would be a problem, and He took care of this issue for us.

*"However, when He, the Spirit of truth, has come, He will guide you into all truth; for He will not speak on His own authority, but whatever He hears He will speak; and He will tell you things to come."* (John 16:13)

God sent the Holy Spirit, whom we also know as the Spirit of truth. In the midst of this discussion, another truth is revealed and made clear. All 7 of these Spirits are manifestations of the Holy Spirit. When you see these seven Spirits before the throne of God in heaven, this is a representation of the complete work of the Holy Spirit. The Holy Spirit is manifested in seven unique ways to meet all the needs we have. It is the Holy Spirit who gives us discernment. It's the Holy Spirit who leads us into truth. You can't truly understand the Bible without the Holy Spirit. The Bible is the truth, and it is the Holy Spirit who guides us into all truth. Therefore, understanding the Bible has to do with discernment. You can only discern it through the work of the Holy Spirit in you.

Try to remember how it was before you received the baptism of the Holy Spirit. Remember how many things in the Bible you read, but just couldn't understand. Remember reading things and saying, "I just don't get it." Think about the time you heard someone talking about a verse, and you said, "I just don't get it." Can you remember hearing a sermon and saying, "I just don't get it." Then after getting baptized in the Holy Spirit, all of a sudden you started to understand those things, and you started saying, "I get it! I get it!" The reason for this is that the Holy Spirit guides us and gives us the discernment we need to understand the Word correctly. The truth is that you just can't understand it correctly without the Spirit of truth.

Discernment differentiates between false and true teachings. In an age of deception, discernment is critical to our survival. Where do you get discernment? There is only one source. You get it from the Holy Spirit. The Holy Spirit has been the sole source for truth since the beginning of time. In fact, in the nine gifts of the Holy Spirit, discernment is one of the very important gifts Paul mentioned.

We have seen much confusion about the gift of discerning of spirits: I hear some people asking for the ability to see little demons at work around them. That may happen if the Holy Spirit thinks it is needed, but I believe that the number one purpose for this gift is to discern the movement and work of the Holy Spirit. It is to help you see and understand the Spirit of Christ that is working with you and for you.

When you know what the real thing is like (through the gift of discernment) you immediately recognize the counterfeit sent in by the enemy. When you know the truth, you immediately recognize the false and the untrue. You begin to immediately recognize any spirit which is not of the truth. When you recognize it, you are enabled by the same Spirit of truth to resist it.

## THERE IS ANOTHER THING YOU MUST KNOW

Everything today has a warning label. I love those commercials that say their medication will help you breath more clearly, but it has a couple of side effects. Side effects like difficulty breathing, gut wrenching trauma, death, and thoughts of suicide. There are just a few little things to be concerned about, but most of the time it makes you breathe better. Have you noticed that most of the medications advertized on TV have these terrible warning labels on them. Well here is a warning label for dealing with the Spirit of truth:

## WHEN THE SPIRIT OF TRUTH COMES
## THE ENEMY WILL RESPOND

When you receive the Spirit of truth, the enemy is going to send the spirit of falsehood against you immediately. These warnings are not new! They have been around a long time. I want you to know that brother Peter knew something about deception when he wrote:

*"They have left the straight way and wandered off to follow the way of Balaam son of Beor, who loved the wages of wickedness. But he was rebuked for his wrongdoing by a donkey—a beast without speech—who spoke with a man's voice and restrained the prophet's madness. These men are springs without water and mists driven by a storm. Blackest darkness is reserved for them."* (2 Peter 2:15-17, NIV)

The spirit of Balaam is the spirit of falsehood. At this point, you need to know an important Biblical truth: You are blessed by God with the blessing of righteous Abraham. But, the spirit of Balaam will try to bring a curse against you. This spirit will come to you and say, "You are not really blessed and I am going to put a curse on you. And when I put this curse on you, you will see that you are not really blessed by God." This is a lie from hell, and you must not accept it.

The spirit of falsehood (the spirit of Balaam) wants to deceive you into thinking that you don't really have the blessing. Many people are actually confessing these lies with their own mouths. They are speaking all these lies into being, and empowering the curses which have come upon them. It seems as if they no longer recognize that they are the blessed children of God. When you confess the lies of the enemy, you open up your hedge of protection, and make yourself more vulnerable to additional enemy attacks. The spirit of Balaam wants you to distrust God's Word. He wants you to believe that the promises of the Word are a lie. This spirit wants you to let go of your blessing and embrace the curse.

The spirit of Balaam is especially effective at getting into people who are opportunistic. I had this wonderful friend in a church I served before going into the military. I really liked this guy. We were in the same Sunday School class, and became close friends. He had the type of personality which made you want to spend time with him and become close friends. He was just a neat, fun guy. He and his wife owned a dog grooming service. They had a mobile unit which they drove out to homes where they could groom pets on site. But, they also had a store where they did most of their dog grooming business. I enjoyed going to the shop and visiting with both of them. The man was fun to be with, and he had a great sense of humor. He was very bright and well educated, and my visits with him were infor-mative as well as entertaining.

Now when I went into his shop (remember that this was a dog grooming business) he had a section in the reception room where you could have monogrammed key chains made. If you moved over to another section, he could make name plates for you. He had another section for bumper stickers. There was another section where you could have ball point pens made with your company name or logo. He had almost every little gimmick you could think up in that one small space. His business was successful and he didn't really need the money from these sideline services. Eventually, I came to understand that he really had an opportunistic spirit.

As I was visiting with him and something was going on in the world (maybe it was in the newspaper or on the TV in the store), he would pick up on that and say, "You know, there has got to be a way to make a buck out of this!" Everything he looked at resulted in the same outcome: "There has got to be a way to make a buck out of this!"

I discovered that there are some people who are like that. They are sort of wired that way. But, one of the dangers for people who are wired this way is that the spirit of Balaam can slip in. Now, this didn't happen to my friend, but for people who are opportunistic, this spirit can easily slip in without their awareness.

Remember and take heed of the words in Jude 11. *"Woe to them! ... have run greedily in the error of Balaam for profit;"*

Now the story of Balaam is one of the funniest stories in the Bible. I truly believe God has a sense of humor, and His inclusion of this story in the Bible proves it for me. Remember in this story about Balaam: Balak, king of Moab, got worried about Israel coming to the border of his land. It is important to note that Israel asked only to walk through their country. They agreed to not even drink a glass of water without paying for it. They said they would not touch anything unless Moab offered to sell it to them, and they would pay a fair price for everything. The leaders of Moab said, "NO!" and they came out with the army to war against Israel.

God had commanded Israel not to do any harm to the Moabites. That was God's plan, and Moses was committed to sticking with the plan. However, Balak was not a wise man. He knew this famous guy (Balaam) who could put real curses on people. So Balak offered Balaam money to curse Israel.

*"Now Balak the son of Zippor saw all that Israel had done to the Amorites. And Moab was exceedingly afraid of the people because they were many, and Moab was sick with dread because of the children of Israel. So Moab said to the elders of Midian, "Now this company will lick up everything around us, as an ox licks up the grass of the field." And Balak the son of Zippor was king of the Moabites at that time. Then he sent messengers to Balaam the son of Beor at Pethor, which is near the River in the land of the sons of his people, to call him, saying: "Look, a people has come from Egypt. See, they cover the face of the earth, and are settling next to me! Therefore please come at once, curse this people for me, for they are too mighty for me. Perhaps I shall be able to defeat them and drive them out of the land, for I know that he whom you bless is blessed, and he whom you curse is cursed." So the elders of Moab and the elders of Midian departed with the diviner's fee in their hand, and they came to Balaam and spoke to him the words of Balak. And he said to them, "Lodge here tonight, and I will bring back word to you, as the Lord speaks to me." So the princes of Moab stayed with Balaam. Then God came to Balaam and said, "Who are these men with you?"* (Numbers 22:2-9)

Have you ever noticed that when God asks a question, He's not really looking for information? There is definitely something more going on here.

> *"So Balaam said to God, "Balak the son of Zippor, king of Moab, has sent to me, saying, 'Look, a people has come out of Egypt, and they cover the face of the earth. Come now, curse them for me; perhaps I shall be able to overpower them and drive them out.'" And God said to Balaam, "You shall not go with them; you shall not curse the people, for they are blessed."* (Numbers 22:10-12)

Balaam clearly heard what God command, but he really wanted that money. Balaam was an opportunistic guy, and he wanted to receive a big fee from the king for his divination services. What Balaam did is what a lot of people do who are influenced by the spirit of falsehood. He began to twist the truth a little bit. Many people will begin to put a little spin on the truth so things will go their way. Look at how Balaam twists the truth of God's word.

> *"And God came to Balaam at night and said to him, "If the men come to call you, rise and go with them; but only the word which I speak to you—that you shall do." So Balaam rose in the morning, saddled his donkey, and went with the princes of Moab.* (Numbers 22:20-21, NKJV)

When I first read this, I didn't see where Balaam was disobedient to God. But Balaam had twisted what God said. He didn't wait for men to come to him. He went with the men who were already there. But, that is not what God told him to do. Balaam was so greedy for the money that he lost his senses and his integrity.

Then God's anger was aroused because he went, and the Angel of the Lord took His stand in the way as an adversary against him. And he was riding on his donkey, and his two servants *were* with him. Now the donkey saw the Angel of the Lord standing in the way with His drawn sword in His hand, and the donkey turned aside out of the way and went into the field. So Balaam struck the donkey to turn her back onto the road. Then the Angel of the Lord stood in a narrow path between the vineyards, *with* a wall on this side and a wall on that side. And when the donkey saw the Angel of the Lord, she pushed herself against the wall and crushed Balaam's foot against the wall; so he struck her again. Then the Angel of the Lord went further, and stood in a narrow place where there *was* no way to turn either to the right hand or to the left. And when the donkey saw the Angel of the Lord, she lay down under Balaam; so Balaam's anger was aroused, and he struck the donkey with his staff. - Numbers 22:22-27

Don't you just love it when your donkey is more spiritually discerning than you are? But, this didn't seem to bother Balaam. All he was thinking about was the money. His greed made him lose any sense of discernment he may have had. So, Balaam beat the Donkey to get it back on the road.

Then the Lord opened the mouth of the donkey, and she said to Balaam, "What have I done to you, that you have struck me these three times?" And Balaam said to the donkey, "Because you have abused me. I wish there were a sword in my hand, for now I would kill you!" So the donkey said to Balaam, "*Am* I not your donkey on which you have ridden, ever since *I became* yours, to this day? Was I ever disposed to do this to you?" And he said, "No."- Numbers 22:28-30

One of the very fascinating parts of this story is that Balaam didn't seem surprised that his donkey was able to talk. Without a hint of shock, he just joined into this long conversation with his donkey. A really good clue here is: If you begin to hear animals talk and find yourself having arguments with them, something more is at play here. It may be time to consider that God is trying to tell you something very important, and you should be listening for the voice of God. But, Balaam went on seemingly unfazed by this encounter with a talking donkey. This is what the spirit of falsehood can do to you. When you are open to this spirit, you will go along with things which would normally seem very foolish to you. This is a very dangerous spirit.

*"Then the Lord opened Balaam's eyes, and he saw the Angel of the Lord standing in the way with His drawn sword in His hand; and he bowed his head and fell flat on his face. And the Angel of the Lord said to him, "Why have you struck your donkey these three times? Behold, I have come out to stand against you, because your way is perverse before Me. The donkey saw Me and turned aside from Me these three times. If she had not turned aside from Me, surely I would also have killed you by now, and let her live." And Balaam said to the Angel of the Lord, "I have sinned, for I did not know You stood in the way against me. Now therefore, if it displeases You, I will turn back." Then the Angel of the Lord said to Balaam, "Go with the men, but only the word that I speak to you, that you shall speak." So Balaam went with the princes of Balak."* (Numbers 22:31-35)

God told Balaam not to put a curse on Israel. However, he wanted the reward and he tried in spite of all God had done to stop him. In addition to the first 2 attempts, Balaam tried 5 more times. He knew he was not supposed to curse them, but he kept trying, because he wanted that money. He had a character defect: He was opportunistic, and the enemy was effectively using it for his advantage.

It would be nice if we could say that poor old Balaam learned his lesson here, but he didn't learn. He was opportunistic to the very end. The story didn't end where Numbers 22 leaves off. You have to go further in the Bible to find the results of Balaam's error and others who fall into falsehood.

> *"And Moses said to them: "Have you kept all the women alive? Look, these women caused the children of Israel, through the counsel of Balaam, to trespass against the Lord in the incident of Peor, and there was a plague among the congregation of the Lord."* (Numbers 31:15-16)

When Balaam couldn't get his money directly through his cursing business, he resorted to deceit and trickery. Balaam broke God's command again. He tricked the people into bringing a curse upon themselves. He convinced Balak that he could weaken them by damaging their relationship with God. Then in their weakened condition Balak might defeat them.

The Bible doesn't say, but I can imagine that he received the money. But, as you will see in later passages, it didn't help him in the long run. You may wonder why we spent all this time on an Old Testament Story. It is because the story didn't end with this ancient historical account. This curse of being led by a spirit of falsehood continued right into the New Testament church.

*Eating the worlds spiritual meats*

> *"Nevertheless, I have a few things against you: You have people there who hold to the teaching of Balaam, who taught Balak to entice the Israelites to sin by eating food sacrificed to idols and by committing sexual immorality."* (Revelation 2:14)

As you can see, this is a message for the church age — it is a warning for us. This spirit entices people away from God through deception. It uses the pleasures of the flesh to tempt you to sin. And today this deception is running rampant in our culture. Things that used to get movies an "X" rating now only warrant a "PG" rating, and many of them are shown on prime time television. Today, we are still following the doctrine of Balaam. Many of the people who own and operate these sin based businesses are members in good standing in churches. There are churches which do not call sin, sin, because they want the income from the offerings and tithes. Like Balaam, they choose money over obedience to God. There is a mortal danger in following our own way.

> *"There is a way that seems right to a man, But its end is the way of death."* (Proverbs 14:12 & 16:25)

When you don't see God's judgment on sin right away, you can become uncertain. When you see people who seemingly get away with sin and even prosper by it, you may become unsure about whether the judgment will ever come. Some people take this as permission to do the same things that others are doing. But, look at what happened to Balaam.

> *"In addition to those slain in battle, the Israelites had put to the sword Balaam son of Beor, who practiced divination."* (Joshua 13:22)

The Word of God makes it clear that our choice between truth and falsehood is literally a life and death decision. When you follow the enemy into temptation, he doesn't care what happens to you. After all, the enemy wants to steal your blessing, kill your soul and body, and destroy your destiny for God. He wins when he leads you into sin and he wins when you die from the results. Don't give in to him! Don't let him win!

# HOW DO YOU DEAL WITH THE SPIRIT OF BALAAM

You must first examine yourself to be certain there is no spirit of falsehood operating in your own life. Many people do not get past this stage because they are unwilling to be tested, or they are unwilling to admit their own mistakes or failures. They don't want to know that they have allowed this spiritual influence to color their lives. But, the truth is that we all have some of the spirit of falsehood operating in our lives. And, we know that to be free and to become more than conquers, we must discover if the enemy is working through us and then deal with it. If we discover that he has found a way to use us to propagate his message of falsehood, we need to seek deliverance before we do battle with him or any of his oppressive spirits. It is imperative to get ourselves free so that we can fight the good fight. Jesus saw this spirit operating in some of the most religious people of His day, and said:

> "*You belong to your father, the devil, and you want to carry out your father's desire. He was a murderer from the beginning, not holding to the truth, for there is no truth in him. When he lies, he speaks his native language, for he is a liar and the father of lies.*" (John 8:44, NIV)

You can't really help someone else until you have overcome these demon spirits in your own life. You can't accurately see these spirits working in others until you get them out of your own life so the veil of deception can be lifted from your eyes. Jesus spoke of this need:

> "*Hypocrite! First remove the plank from your own eye, and then you will see clearly to remove the speck from your brother's eye.*" (Matthew 7:5)

The next skill you need to develop is to stop listening to the voice of the enemy, no matter who it comes through! Don't listen to his lies. If you start listening to lies, you will get caught up in them and start rationalizing and twisting things. As you listen to his lies, you will begin to fall into deception. You must learn to recognize his tactics, and break free from his influence. You need to understand that he is trying to destroy you, and he always lies as do all his followers. He will lie to you and he will lie about you. He will send people you know and trust to tell you these lies. To continue to stand, you must open up to the Spirit of truth who will guide you into all truth and out of his lies. Remember Paul's instruction in Romans 10:17: *"So then faith comes by hearing, and hearing by the word of God."* If faith comes by hearing the Word of God, how do we pick up spirits of fear, judgment, and condemnation? These all come from hearing the words of the enemy. So, don't listen to him!

Next, you need to stop going with the flow of the world. Refrain from going along with groups simply because others are going that way. The enemy uses this natural tendency to lure us into deception.

*"For the time will come when men will not put up with sound doctrine. Instead, to suit their own desires, they will gather around them a great number of teachers to say what their itching ears want to hear. They will turn their ears away from the truth and turn aside to myths."* (2 Timothy 4:3-4, NIV)

We were created to be social, and it is good to have friends. It is good to live in harmony and cooperation with others. What the enemy likes to do is take a strength to the extreme and turn it into a weakness by getting you to push it too far. People are then tempted to go along with evil in order to keep the peace or to keep good relationships with people. They do things because everyone else is doing them rather than because it is true and right. When you do that, you fall right into the trap.

One of the most challenging parts of being a disciples is being one of those who is "called forth." The Greek word translated "church" is actually a word meaning "called forth." It means that times will come when you have to stand alone. There will be times when your friends will separate from you, because they don't want to go the way you are going. Disciples have to remain ready and willing to go through those times knowing that the Lord will bring others into their lives who will bless and build them up. You must always remain aware of who you are and whose you are.

The Apostle John said, *"But you have an anointing from the Holy One, and all of you know the truth."* (1 John 2:20, NIV) Through this anointing you have come to know the truth, and one of those truths is that you have been consecrated (set apart) unto and for God's purposes.

The enemy attempts to attack the anointing, and he will tempt you to attack the anointing in someone else. He wants to distort the truth about you and he wants you to join with him in distorting the truth about others. Because of this, we live in this delicate balance: to be social and harmonious, yet not blindly following the crowd.

You need the full protection of the Spirit of truth to stand your ground against your ancient enemy, the devil. He is dedicated to his cause and works tirelessly to distort the truth and veil the eyes of the world. You need the whole armor of God in order to continue standing.

*"Finally, my brethren, be strong in the Lord and in the power of His might. Put on the whole armor of God, that you may be able to stand against the wiles of the devil. For we do not wrestle against flesh and blood, but against principalities, against powers, against the*

*rulers of the darkness of this age, against spiritual hosts of wickedness in the heavenly places. Therefore take up the whole armor of God, that you may be able to withstand in the evil day, and having done all, to stand."* (Ephesians 6:10-13)

Have you noticed that the first item of armor is the "belt of truth." This should be a clue about the importance of having the Spirit of truth working in your life, your ministry, and in your church, because everything else depends on the truth. Without the truth you can't hold the rest of it together. But God never leaves you defenseless. He sends the Spirit of truth. He does this, because He knows that without the truth you cannot stand.

It takes a group effort to deal with the spirit of falsehood. It is critically important to stand together against this extremely deceptive spirit. You need to support your pastor and other leaders as they take their stand for truth and against falsehood. Together you can overcome it. With the help of the Spirit of truth, you can cast out this awful spirit of deception. This is a life and death crisis. If you don't cast this spirit of falsehood out, the enemy may be able to accomplish his purpose and literally kill you. That is what happened to the original person manifesting the spirit of falsehood. If you stop reading the story in the book of Numbers, you will miss the important conclusion to this message about the spirit of Balaam. It cost Balaam his life. What is the value of money if it costs you your life?

*"In addition to those slain in battle, the Israelites had put to the sword Balaam son of Beor, who practiced divination."* (Joshua 13:22, NIV)

As you take a second look at this passage from Joshua, notice that dealing with Balaam was a group effort by Israel!

You can only cast this spirit out if you agree to do it together. And as you serve the Lord you must remember that these wicked spirits mentioned early in the Bible have not gone away, and they have not died. Balaam is mentioned again in Nehemiah, Micah, 2 Peter, Jude, and Revelation. This is not some ancient story without relevance for today. The spirit of Balaam (spirit of falsehood) is alive and well in the world and in the church. He is just as devious and destructive today as he was in Moses' time. Therefore, you must take your stand against him.

## TO PLEASE GOD, YOU MUST BE FAITHFUL TO THE TRUTH.

In his third letter, John says it over and over, "walk in the truth, walk in the truth, walk in the truth.

*"It gave me great joy to have some brothers come and tell about your faithfulness to the truth and how you continue to walk in the truth. I have no greater joy than to hear that my children are walking in the truth."* (3 John 1:3-4, NIV)

If John got so much joy from their faithfulness, what about the Lord's joy? I believe that one day we would all like to hear something like this: *"His lord said to him, 'Well done, good and faithful servant; you were faithful over a few things, I will make you ruler over many things. Enter into the joy of your lord."* (Matthew 25:21 & 23) But, the real question is: Are you willing to pay the price now to hear Him say that later? Are you willing to pay the price even if it means losing some friends? Are you willing to pay the price even if it means having some family members distance themselves from you? Are you willing to stand for the truth even if you can't get that business deal or you lose some of your work benefits? Or, are you opportunistic, like Balaam, to the point that you would let go of the truth to gain the wealth of the world?

What is more important to you: the approval of man or the approval of God? This is a question we must answer, and the answer is a matter of life and death. Paul urged Timothy to do his best to be approved of God.

*"Be diligent to present yourself approved to God, a worker who does not need to be ashamed, rightly dividing the word of truth."* (2 Timothy 2:15)

Paul reminds Timothy and all disciples of Jesus Christ that to please God, you have to correctly handle the word of truth. You know that this is all that teachers, parents, and leaders can do. You can teach, you can urge, and you can pray. But, ultimately the decision rests with each individual. Do you stand in the truth or not? Do you follow the Spirit of truth or the spirit of falsehood?

As you continue to learn and consider the lessons in this boot-camp, I want you to know that now is the time to develop your combat skills. After the bullets start flying, it's too late for practice.

In the "Left behind" movie, Rayford comes home to find that his wife and son have disappeared along with millions of others. His daughter is away at college, and he doesn't know what has happened to her. In his frustration and anger, he begins to break things in his bedroom. He throws his wife's Bible into a mirror which breaks into a million pieces. After his anger dies down, he picks up the Bible, wipes away the broken glass, and opens it to Genesis 1:1 and reads, "In the beginning." He pauses for a moment to reflect and then says, *"It's a little late for that..."*

When you are in the heat of the battle, and enemy fire is hitting all around you, it is a little too late to begin reading the Bible. So you need to get ready now and stay ready. The only way to be ready is through sword drills, now. You may remember that the Sword of the Spirit is the Word of God.

like building a house in a storm

When you search for scriptures which provide you with power statements to use against the enemy in your spiritual warfare, you are doing sword drills. Storing the Word in your heart is like sharpening a sword and making it ready for battle.

Practice on small temptations before you go after the big ones. You can begin by resisting inappropriate suggestions. If you think that something is inappropriate to watch, then it is probably inappropriate to watch and you should turn it off. If your friends are going somewhere, and it seems inappropriate for you to be there, it is probably inappropriate. Don't go! Remember, you are not alone. God is with you and He has sent help for you. So, you need to daily seek guidance from the Spirit of Truth!

Remember what God said through Jesus, "I am giving you the Spirit of truth forever." That is why every morning I ask the Holy Spirit what heaven is saying today. I want to know every morning before I launch out into the day what will please Father God, bless the Lord Jesus, and not grieve the Holy Spirit. This is such an awesomely powerful Spirit, and He is with you all day, every day. You need to learn now how to work with the Holy Spirit in order to become combat ready.

Being combat ready is about adopting the core competencies of a true warrior. Being led by the Spirit of truth is one of those core competencies. Get it working for you now, and keep it working forever.

## PRAYER FOR THE SPIRIT OF TRUTH

Father God, I ask today that you would impart to us a greater willingness to cooperate with the Spirit of truth, which you have already given us. Father God, we thank you for sending the Spirit of truth. And Lord God let us open our spiritual ears to hear what the Spirit is saying. Lord God, help us so that we may put on the whole armor every day, and be prepared to stand. And, when we have done everything to stand (even if the whole world turns against us — when we have done everything to stand) may we keep on standing for Jesus. May we keep on standing in and for the truth! May we resist the spirit of Balaam, the spirit of falsehood, and stand with you forever and ever!

Father God, help us. Here we are. Use us as we give ourselves to you. We submit to you spirit, soul, and body. We resist the enemy and we declare by your Word that he must flee from us and take all his works with him as we stand with you in the truth. We pray it Lord, in the mighty name of Yeshua ha Messiach. Amen and amen!

## NOTES

# LESSON 3

# "THE SPIRIT OF HOLINESS"

In military organizations, the process of determining if people should move up in rank begins almost immediately after their arrival in the unit. Many are thrust into positions of leadership who would not have chosen it for themselves. Some are offered leadership positions, and readily accept the opportunity to serve. Others are driven from within themselves to seek leadership positions for their own personal ego needs or to exercise power over others. We have all had experiences with these three different types of individuals, and have our own individual opinions about which of these three methods of selecting leaders is more admirable.

Early in my military career, a young private came to see me. He was under great stress and was almost at his wits end. Another soldier was caught up in his own sense of being in a superior leadership position and was abusing his authority. He had this young soldier shining his boots and making his bed. The soldier believed that he was required to do that because the other person outranked him. I asked about the other soldier's rank and had to fight to suppress laughter when I found out that the other soldier had been a private for one day longer than the soldier in my office. I was amazed that anyone would look at date of rank to determine which private was superior to another.

This young soldier was greatly relieved when I informed him that only people in key command positions and general officers have personal aides to do some of their tasks, and even those tasks are limited.

Moses was caught up in a very difficult dilemma. He had reluctantly been thrust into leadership by the Lord. This had happened over his many protests and in spite of all the reasons he gave for not accepting the position. On the other hand, Korah, Dathan, and Abiram lusted after power, and attempted to thrust themselves into Moses' leadership position. This passage of scripture offers up many lessons about leadership in the church. In this account, we are given insight to enable us to discern the ugliness of the lust for power and the terrible consequences which can come to someone who violates the calling and anointing of God.

This third week of training struck me as a time to focus on young people and especially those in their teen years. Every day they live in the midst of a great spiritual battle zone in which many are deceived by the enemy. Others are deceived by teachers who are pushing political agendas more than imparting the basic educational lessons. Still others are facing the deception of peer group members who would lead them into rebellion, and tantalize them with the allure of drugs and alcohol which are so readily available to them today. A few years ago, the world seemed much safer for young people. Now, they are thrust into combat zones where they must develop the wisdom of the street in order to survive the constant enemy attacks.

An awareness of being set apart for God is a powerful answer to the dilemma they face each day while attempting to stay pure and righteous in an unholy arena. They are daily exposed to people who are seeking disciples for their evolutionary theories denying the existence of God. Others in their peer group attempt to recruit them into the popular culture of substance abuse, violence, and immorality. Our young people need our support, our prayers, and our wisdom to help them navigate through these very dangerous waters. Their situation and challenges remind us of one theme in this training; "Like it or not, we are engaged in spiritual warfare!" The danger faced by our youth makes it even more important for the church to hear, to understand, and to support them in their daily battles.

Our ancient enemy, the devil, is daily waging spiritual warfare with each of us. He would like to steal this generation of our youth, kill their hopes and dreams for the future, and destroy their destiny in the Lord. His objective is clearly stated by Jesus, and whether you like it or not, he is coming after you. Whether you want to fight or not, he has already picked a life or death fight with you. He is coming after you whether you like it or not. So, pay close attention to what Jesus is saying.

*"The thief does not come except to steal, and to kill, and to destroy. I have come that they may have life, and that they may have it more abundantly."* (John 10:10)

To survive, you must learn how to wage spiritual warfare. You need to be in the process of training, staying alert, and maintaining readiness. To do this, you must constantly keep yourself informed, and be committed to training the next generation. They need mature believers to teach them how to fight the good fight of faith while remaining in the love and grace of God. They need to become full members of the Body of Christ which is now His end-time army of spiritual warriors.

Thomas Jefferson said, *"The price of freedom is eternal vigilance."* This lesson about freedom seems to be one which must be learned through the experiences of each generation. I have a hope that this knowledge will become transferable and something you can use to impart the next generation. I pray that our youth will be enabled to avoid the terrible price which must be paid when you let down your guard, and let the enemy in your camp where he can wage such destructive warfare against you. Peter remembered the words of warning which Jesus gave him, but it was too late. He remember the lesson after his great fall and subsequent restoration. Peter wrote:

*"Be self-controlled and alert. Your enemy the devil prowls around like a roaring lion looking for someone to devour."* (1 Peter 5:8, NIV)

Have you noticed in this passage that the enemy is not really a lion, but he tries to act like one? It is a lie! But if you believe it and start living in fear, you will give him an opening through which he can attack you. Remember that the real lion is the Lion of the Tribe of Judah. The real lion is Yeshua ha Messiach. The real Lion of Judah defeated the enemy on the cross. So, don't let him fool you like he fooled Peter on the night Jesus was arrested.

That night, Peter met the enemy face to face, and discovered too late that he was unprepared for the fight. Fear replaced faith, and in a moment of weakness he denied ever having known the Lord Jesus. At that point he must have remembered Jesus saying, *"Therefore whoever confesses Me before men, him I will also confess before My Father who is in heaven. But whoever denies Me before men, him I will also deny before My Father who is in heaven."* (Matthew 10:32-33) On another occasion Jesus said, *"Also I say to you, whoever confesses Me before men, him the Son of Man also will confess before the angels of God. But he who denies Me before men will be denied before the angels of God."* (Luke 12:8-9)

If you don't want to pay the price Peter paid, you must be sure that you don't fall for the enemy's deception. The devil is not a lion! He is a defeated foe. Don't believe his lies or fall for his tricks. He only has the power you give him. So, don't listen to him. Listen to what the Word of God is saying.

*"You shall tread upon the lion and the cobra, The young lion and the serpent you shall trample under-*

*foot. 'Because he has set his love upon Me, therefore I will deliver him; I will set him on high, because he has known My name. He shall call upon Me, and I will answer him; I will be with him in trouble; I will deliver him and honor him. With long life I will satisfy him, And show him My salvation.'"* (Psalm 91:13-16)

Remember who is on your side! Remember who will always stand up for you. Remember who will stand by you, and be closer to you than a brother. When you go to war, you need to know who is on your side. You want to know who the friendly forces are, and who you can count on in the heat of the battle. Young people need to know that their parents are with them, their grandparents are with them, and their church is with them. They need to know that all of these will pray for them and support them. They need to know that they have even more than this on their side. Help them to know that Jesus is on their side, and God is the main element available to them among their friendly forces. I recommend that your study, memorize, and take to heart the promises of Psalm 91 which is often called the "Warrior's Psalm." Pay particular attention to verses 13-16, because these promises will help you with your estimate of friendly forces.

God says that you "shall tread upon the lion." The destiny of every young person in Christ is to tread on the lion and the cobra. Through you, God will fulfill His promise to Eve in the garden when he decreed that her seed would crush the head of the serpent. Notice in Psalm 91 that God promises to rescue you because you love Him. When you are in danger or in trouble, all you have to do is acknowledge God and love Him. When someone comes after you or when you are threatened, all you have to do is say, "Jesus!" When you acknowledge Jesus, your circumstances change and the power of God is shifted to your side. God promises that when you call upon Him, He will answer you. He promises to be with you, deliver you, and honor you with long life. God never leaves you defenseless. He gives you weapons of warfare.

You can have confidence in what God will do, because you have his published plan; His OPERATIONS ORDER. His entire plan has been published for centuries. It is the Bible. In addition, it is the powerful sword of the Spirit. When you study, understand, and memorize the Word of God it is stored in your heart and can be drawn out when you need it. Jesus did this when He had to face Satan. After only three thrusts of that sword, the devil decided to leave and wait for a more opportune time. He thought he might find a time when Jesus was not as sharp or well prepared to draw that sword and use it. Remember James 4:7, "Therefore submit to God. Resist the devil and he will flee from you." All you have to do is resist the devil and he will flee from you.

In addition to the sword, Jesus provided other very powerful weapons of warfare. This takes us back to the primary text of this study.

*"And I looked, and behold, in the midst of the throne and of the four living creatures, and in the midst of the elders, stood a Lamb as though it had been slain, having seven horns and seven eyes, which are the seven Spirits of God sent out into all the earth."* (Revelation 5:6)

You see clearly in this passage that God has sent these seven spirits out to fight with and for each of you and your young people. We need to speak this Word over them, and speak it into them until it becomes fixed and certain in their hearts and lives. They have these seven powerful weapons, but to make them effective, they need to learn how to use them.

In the previous two lessons, you have learned about two of the seven Spirits of God. We first looked at the Spirit of Wisdom and Revelation. Who comes against it? Jezebel! Next, we went into some depth to study about the ministry of the

Spirit of Truth. Who comes against it? It is the spirit of falsehood or the spirit of Balaam.

In this lesson, we are looking at the Spirit of holiness. Remember that many of the translators saw that these spirits were definitely the work of the Holy Spirit and capitalized the word Spirit. Paul makes mention of the Spirit of holiness in the book of Romans.

*"Paul, a bondservant of Jesus Christ, called to be an apostle, separated to the gospel of God which He promised before through His prophets in the Holy Scriptures, concerning His Son Jesus Christ our Lord, who was born of the seed of David according to the flesh, and declared to be the Son of God with power according to the Spirit of holiness, by the resurrection from the dead."* (Romans 1:1-4)

According to this passage, the Spirit of holiness has power. Paul says the Spirit of holiness declared with power. In fact it was this Spirit who declared with power and raised Jesus from the dead. When someone has been dead for three days, it takes awesome power to raise that person with all the parts of the body working effectively. There was no brain damage and none of his body was in decomposition. That is significant power, and it all came through the declaration of the Spirit of Holiness.

## IT IS CRITICALLY IMPORTANT
## TO UNDERSTAND HOLINESS

Many churches and teachers simply avoid this topic because of past errors and misunderstandings. However, ignoring the topic does not solve any of the problems. The writer of Hebrews makes a startling declaration:

*"Make every effort to live in peace with all men and to be holy; without holiness no one will see the Lord."* (Hebrews 12:14, NIV)

Without holiness, you will not see the Lord. Without holiness, you cannot please the Lord. As Paul writes in Romans 8:8 (NIV), *"Those controlled by the sinful nature cannot please God."* You must also remember that you cannot earn holiness or achieve it through your works of righteousness. Jesus is the only source for holiness. 1 Corinthians 1:30 (NIV), *"It is because of him that you are in Christ Jesus, who has become for us wisdom from God—that is, our righteousness, holiness and redemption."*

To truly understand this concept, you need to separate Biblical holiness from the English word holiness. I looked for the definition of holiness in Webster's dictionary. It was defined as: "the quality of being holy" or "a title for the pope." The English word "holiness" is a poor word to translate the original Hebrew and Greek. It simply does not convey the real meaning of these words.

The Hebrew word translated as holiness is "qadosh" which means devoted or dedicated to a particular purpose.

The Greek word for holiness is "hagiasos" which means separated unto God or set apart for God.

Holiness is not about the quality of your spirit, but about the Lord to whom you have dedicated your life and separated yourself from the world. Holiness means that you are no longer living according to the standards of the world, but you are now living unto the Lord in order to live for Him and to live up to His standards. When this happens, you are no longer just part of the crowd. You have been set apart for some special purpose. It doesn't necessarily mean that you are better than others. It means that God has chosen you in His grace for His purpose.

In the Bible, people, places, objects and days can be holy if they have been set apart for God or for His service. The temple;

the gold in the temple; and the priests were called holy. The Sabbath is holy, because it is set apart by God for Him and His rest. Israel was a holy nation because it was set apart by God for His purpose of blessing the entire world.

Given this definition, begin to think of this word, "*holiness*," in terms of the five-fold ministry. Today, holiness has primarily to do with the five-fold offices of ministry; those who have been set apart for the purpose of ministering to God's people. Look closely at Paul's teaching in the fourth chapter of the book of Ephesians:

> "*It was he who gave some to be apostles, some to be prophets, some to be evangelists, and some to be pastors and teachers, to prepare God's people for works of service, so that the body of Christ may be built up until we all reach unity in the faith and in the knowledge of the Son of God and become mature, attaining to the whole measure of the fullness of Christ.*" (Ephesians 4:11-13, NIV)

Paul is saying that some people are being set apart for a specific work of the Lord. When these people are set apart by the Lord for the work of ministry, they become holy unto the Lord. They are not holy because within themselves they are pure, good, perfect, and righteous or because they have done all the right things without making mistakes. The Lord is calling these individuals and setting them apart, gifting them for the work, and anointing them for His purpose. And, it is this work of the Lord which sets them apart, and thereby makes them holy unto the Lord.

God's purpose is to prepare people for service. That is what the Priests and Levites were supposed to do. They were set apart for the Lord and were supposed to teach the people how to serve God. Therefore they became holy. Not every Levite was allowed to serve in every capacity. The callings were very specific. Not every Priest had the same tasks. Each was assigned as God chose when He set them apart. We can understand from this that not everyone is an Apostle. Not everyone is a Prophet. Like the priests and Levites, we do not choose. We do not determine our calling or establish our own anointing. If we get jealous and try to step into someone else's anointing we may be judged as Aaron and Miriam were. We must hold these things in respect and honor the Lord if we are to continue in His blessing.

God's purpose in setting people apart was made clear by Paul in Ephesians 4:12 when he stated: "*so that the body of Christ may be built up.*" This setting apart is always for a purpose. In this case, it is for the purpose of building up the body of Christ. Therefore, those in the five-fold offices of ministry are holy unto the Lord. It is important to know that the Spirit of holiness does this work of setting people apart for ministry.

Consider this carefully. If the Lord is the head and we are the body, does God want a weak, sick, tired, confused, or broken body? No! So, to help us become built up and fully equipped, the Lord has called forth certain people who are assigned the task of building up the church so that we become a healthy functioning body for Jesus. And, this is the reason for the five-fold offices of ministry.

Looking back to the Old Testament, we see that Moses, Aaron, and Miriam were set apart by God for His purposes. Each of them had a unique role and a specific calling in line with God's purpose. Each had been anointed by God for their unique purpose. Moses was anointed to lead. This was the equivalent of being set apart in the apostolic anointing. Aaron was anointed to minister to the Lord and perform all the priestly duties of the ceremonial law. We can look at this as an anointing for a pastor or teacher. Miriam was a prophetess, song writer, and worship leader for the congregation of God's people. Each of them was set apart by God for those unique purposes, and no others could step into their place without God's calling. It didn't go well for Aaron and Miriam when they became jealous and tried to step into Moses' anointing. They had to pay dearly for their rebellious actions.

God gave awesome power and great favor to support them in carrying out His divine purpose for the people. When the Lord told Moses to go to Pharaoh, he didn't feel qualified. He was asking, "Who am I to do something like this?" Moses had a past in Egypt. He had killed an Egyptian and was forced to flee Egypt. There had been a bounty on his life. In addition, he seemed to have some sort of speech impediment. As Moses looked at all these things, he felt totally unqualified for the job. The scriptures even say that Moses was the most humble man on earth. Yet, the Lord made Moses like a god in the eyes of Pharaoh, and he had power to work the signs and wonders of God in order to persuade Pharaoh to let God's people go. God gave Moses the power and authority to part the Red Sea by holding up his staff. When Moses held up that staff, the Israelites triumphed over their enemies. When he smote the rock, water flowed from the stone. These signs and wonders served to prove to the people that when God set them apart, they were uniquely holy unto the Lord. This anointing was sacred, and no one was allowed to move into it on his or her own. You must never presume to step into someone else's anointing.

## THE ENEMY RESPONDES TO THE SPIRIT OF HOLINESS

When the Spirit of Holiness comes and God tells you that He is going to set you apart for a purpose, He gives you the spiritual gifts to accomplish His work. And, when you accept what God is doing in your life, the enemy will respond. The enemy will respond every time the Spirit of holiness comes. And, there is a specific spirit the enemy uses each and every time in order to come against the Spirit of holiness.

When the Spirit of holiness established Moses in power and authority, the ancient enemy, the devil, sent a demonic spirit against Moses to block or hinder his ability to carry out the Lord's purpose for the people. He sent that spirit into some leaders who had character defects and were open to demonic oppression. They were like the army private declaring power because of his date of rank. Four men under the influence of a demonic principality rose up in rebellion and challenged Moses' authority to lead. Korah, Dathan, Abiram, and On tried to set themselves apart as holy when they confronted Moses.

*"Korah son of Izhar, the son of Kohath, the son of Levi, and certain Reubenites—Dathan and Abiram, sons of Eliab, and On son of Peleth—became insolent and rose up against Moses. With them were 250 Israelite men, well-known community leaders who had been appointed members of the council."* (Numbers 16:1-2, NIV)

Have you ever noticed that rebellious people always gather others in support of their cause. Korah is the obvious ringleader of this group of insolent and rebellious men. He is so identified with this spirit that in the New Testament this type of rebellion is referred to as the "rebellion of Korah." His first move was to get other key leaders of notable families to join with him. Then the four of them gathered others to rally behind their cause. Korah had a character defect and he sought out others with the same character defect. All of them had an unholy craving or lust for power and authority that was not rightfully theirs. They were not gifted, anointed, or blessed to be mature leaders whose first priority was obedience to God. They were not concerned with the welfare of the people. They were only motivated by a selfish and wicked desire for power.

The name of Korah became associated with this very wicked spirit that worked through him. It is the spirit of rebellion. People today, who have this same character defect, do the same things Korah did. When we see this happen, we know that the spirit of Korah has found their weakness and has exploited that character defect in order to work through them. People today, under the influence of that spirit will act just like Korah and his rebellious gang. The enemy doesn't have to change the game plan, because people keep falling for it. Believers just don't seem to be able to stay alert and watch for it. They don't learn the lessons of the past so that they can quickly diagnose the problem and apply the proper solution from the Lord.

You see this rebellious spirit in people who become dissatisfied with a ministry. Instead of praying and seeking God's help, they begin to gather people around them and start to discount and marginalize the person who is carrying the true anointing from the Lord. If they can't have their way, they will leave the church, but not without doing their best to take others with them.

In one of the churches I planted, a man did this. He gathered people together in rebellion and they left the church. But, they didn't leave until they had done all the damage they knew how to do. You need to be careful not to go along with this spirit of rebellion, because the same people who joined with you will soon turn against you. A rebellious and contentious spirit is not easily removed. The man who did this actually had the audacity to come to me in tears because those who left with him had turned against him. He wanted me to minister to his grief and loss, but he couldn't grasp that it was the spirit of rebellion working in him, and it would continue until that spirit was cast out.

Before this rebellion occured, someone from another church where he had done the same thing sent a message to me saying, "You are going to be so happy and relieved when he is gone." But, this spirit doesn't just go away after it has found a good host. It will lead the person from church to church or group to group doing the same damage everywhere it goes. I personally witnessed this happening to four different groups this one man participated in, and he never took responsibility or sought help to break free from this rebellious spirit.

The enemy seeks out weak people to go against God's anointed leaders. It is the weak people who often get hurt the most, because they have been enticed to go against what God is doing. They have been deceived into stepping outside their place of blessing and protection. In these times of vulnerability the same enemy who is using them for his rebellion will turn and strike them in order to steal their blessing, kill their hopes and dreams, and destroy their effectiveness for the Lord. In a rebellion, everyone loses. Unlike suffering for the Lord which brings blessings, this kind of suffering only gets worse until they turn back to the Lord in repentance and humbly seek and accept His restoration.

One of the things experience teaches us is that this spirit works in those who do not have the strength in the Holy Spirit which they claim. For a time they seem to be anointed leaders. But, this comes from a counterfeit spirit and it does not last. Those who fall for this and seek to lead a rebellion are usually cowardly people who need others around them to give them the courage to do what the spirit of rebellion is enticing them to do in the church. When they have gathered enough support, they will usually come after the pastor, because it is the five-fold ministry they seek to destroy.

Notice that Korah gathered the well-known community leaders. *"With them were 250 Israelite men, well-known community leaders who had been appointed members of the council."* (Numbers 16:2, NIV) One version of the Bible describes them as people of *"renown."* They were well known and people thought it was safe to follow them. It works the same today when a man or woman steps forward to lead a rebellion in the church. They will try to get the elders and deacons to join with them in a rebellion against the pastor. You will see this over and over again. Every time the Spirit of holiness comes, the spirit of rebellion moves right in behind God's Spirit. Someone will rise up in rebellion, attempt to build a power base of support, and then strive to eliminate those through whom God is working

You can clearly see it when people try to put themselves into an anointed position already occupied by someone who is truly set apart by the Lord. They try to call themselves into this anointing and declare themselves to be as holy as the person in the position. The people who do this are the most dangerous members in the church.

I have frequently heard the objection at this point, "But, some leaders and pastors are wrong, aren't they? Isn't it appropriate for us to move to eliminate leaders and pastors who are in the wrong?" This sounds good at first, and it is true that some leaders and pastors get out of line, but you need to let God deal with them. The Lord is probably less concerned about the problem you think you see in them than He is about the spirit of Korah He sees in you. It is always good and right to pray for people. Pray for your leaders. If you think they are out of line, pray for God to get them back on track. Pray for the Holy Spirit to come in greater power through the Spirit of holiness and touch and help your leaders. Praying against someone or rebelling against the Lord's anointed does not get blessed. God is not with you in a rebellious movement. You will quickly learn the hard way that you are working against God, and He will stop that one way or another. He will stop you; sometimes in alarming ways. He may even remove you to bring stability back to the church.

Armed with this information, notice what Korah and the rebels said to Moses. Look at how they came against him, and what evidence they used to accuse him before the people.

*"They gathered together against Moses and Aaron, and said to them, "You take too much upon yourselves, for all the congregation is holy, every one of them, and the*

*Lord is among them. Why then do you exalt yourselves above the assembly of the Lord?"* (Numbers 16:3)

Did you catch the drift of that accusation: "Who do you think you are? You've gone too far! We are as good as you are! We are as holy as you are, Moses! So, why did you set yourself apart?" They accused Moses of putting himself into the leadership position, but it was God who selected Moses. God had been working with Moses for a long time. Remember how the Lord had him protected in the little basket when he was a baby, and how Pharaoh's daughter found him and brought him into the palace where he could be educated and prepared to lead. God had been with him for 40 years while he served as a shepherd learning the skills to care for God's flock of sheep. God worked with Moses for 80 years before He called to him from the burning bush and put great authority in his hands. Moses didn't set himself apart. God did it.

But, Korah and his followers were saying, "We're just as holy as you are!" "We can do what you do. We can move into your position." You see this all the time in churches. People will say, "Who does that pastor think he is? I can do what he does. In fact, I can do it better than he does. I'll put myself in that role and we'll just get rid of him." That is how the spirit of Korah works in many churches today.

But think about Korah and his followers for a few moments. Think about what they had seen God doing through Moses. They had seen Moses walk back into Egypt at 80 years of age with that staff in his hand. They witnessed it when Moses raised that staff in his hand and the Lord brought the 10 plagues on Egypt. They personally saw all God had released on Egypt through Moses. They had seen him bring a pharaoh to his knees. They had seen the Red Sea parted by Moses, and walked across on dry land. Korah and his followers had seen that. And, when they got to the other side, the people panicked because Pharaoh and the army went into the sea in hot pursuit. Then, they watched as Moses raised that staff again and the waters came in on the Egyptian army giving the people a total victory over their oppressors. Korah tasted the water that came out of a rock in sufficient quantity to satisfy two million people. Korah had eaten the manna which came down from heaven. Korah and his followers had seen Moses call on God to send meat, and quail came in so thick that they were knee deep in the meat. After seeing all that first hand, how foolish can you be to come against all of this power and authority?

Please understand that when you force your way into an anointed position, you can pick any stick you want, decorate it, and embellish it to look good, but nothing is going to happen. The power was not in the stick. Unless God puts that staff into your hand, it is useless. God had given it to Moses, and it was not transferable at that time to anyone else.

After witnessing all these signs and wonders the Lord had worked through Moses, Korah rose up in rebellion. There is no wisdom in this spirit of rebellion and there is no wisdom of the Lord in those who allow this spirit to control them. The spirit of rebellion always comes against those who are being moved by the Spirit of holiness, and it especially likes to come against the apostolic. Even though it specifically targets the apostolic, the spirit of Korah will come against anyone who is moving in the power of the Spirit of holiness. Know this, if God calls you and sets you apart, the spirit of Korah will come against you. Don't act surprised! Don't get caught off guard. Don't act as if it is something new. Remember Peter's warning. Be alert. Be ready, because you know it is coming.

## HOW DO YOU DEAL WITH THE SPIRIT OF KORAH?

The first thing you do is examine yourself to see if there is any part of the spirit of rebellion in you. Being face down before the Lord is always a good posture during self exami- nation. If you see that you have a tendency to rebel against

God's established and anointed authority, you should repent and return to following God's plan as it is executed through His servants. You can't accurately see what is being manifest through others until you first purge it from yourself.

What do you do when that spirit of rebellion comes against you or someone in your church? My advice is that you follow the pattern of Moses.

> *"So when Moses heard it, he fell on his face; and he spoke to Korah and all his company, saying, 'Tomorrow morning the Lord will show who is His and who is holy, and will cause him to come near to Him. That one whom He chooses He will cause to come near to Him. Do this: Take censers, Korah and all your company; put fire in them and put incense in them before the Lord tomorrow, and it shall be that the man whom the Lord chooses is the holy one. You take too much upon yourselves, you sons of Levi!'"* (Numbers 16:4-7)

First, notice what Moses did not do. He didn't pick up the staff and use it against them. He didn't argue with them and point to his own calling. He didn't go through stories of God's working through him to prove that somehow he was right. He didn't challenge them directly. If he had gotten into a big argument with them, the enemy would have used that opportunity to bring other spirits in to do further damage to the people. So, Moses fell face down. What happened while he was face down? In falling face down, he submitted to God. Face down is a position of submission. So, he got himself into proper alignment with God. He resisted the devil. What happens when you submit to God and resist the devil? He must flee from you (see James 4:7).

Then, Moses sought God's answer. He inquired about what God wanted to do. And Moses let Godly Wisdom dictate his response. He let God decide what to do. Notice how Korah responded. When Moses told him what God wanted, Korah refused two times. He was rebellious to the very end. A rebellious spirit is like that all the time. If they rebel and you give them their way, they are likely to say, "No! I'm not going to do it. I'm a rebellious spirit and I rebel all the time. I'm not going to do anything you tell me to do even if it is what I want."

Another clear sign that God was with Moses was given to the people when the earth opened and Korah, his followers, and their families were swallowed up alive into the grave. I heard someone say that they were raptured straight to hell that day. Let's take a closer look at what happened on that day.

> *"And the Lord spoke to Moses and Aaron, saying, "Separate yourselves from among this congregation, that I may consume them in a moment." Then they fell on their faces, and said, "O God, the God of the spirits of all flesh, shall one man sin, and You be angry with all the congregation?" So the Lord spoke to Moses, saying, "Speak to the congregation, saying, 'Get away from the tents of Korah, Dathan, and Abiram.'"* (Numbers 16:20-24)

Think about what would be going through your mind at a moment like that. After all you had seen Moses do, wouldn't you expect that he could do this too? Wouldn't you begin to move away as far as you could get from the tents of the rebellious? Most of the people moved away from their tents, but the rebellious ones remained rebellious. Then Moses told them how the Lord planned to resolve this issue.

> *"And Moses said: "By this you shall know that the Lord has sent me to do all these works, for I have not done them of my own will. If these men die naturally like all men, or if they are visited by the common fate of all men, then the Lord has not sent me. But if the Lord creates a*

*new thing, and the earth opens its mouth and swallows them up with all that belongs to them, and they go down alive into the pit, then you will understand that these men have rejected the Lord."* (Numbers 16:28-30)

In this passage of Scripture, we see the real issue. When you rebel against God's anointed authority, you are treating God with contempt. When Moses made this declaration, the people started stepping back away from Korah and all that belonged to him. His rebellion brought a curse on everything he owned and everyone associated with him. As the whole congregation looked on, the ground opened and Korah and all of his followers, whether they came out that day or not, were swallowed alive and the ground covered over them. When the people heard their screams as they went down to the grave alive, they fled in terror.

However, the 250 men who were burning incense before the Lord in their bronze censors kept going in rebellion. In a flash they were consumed by fire from the Lord. The only thing left were smoldering remains and the 250 censors. The Lord told Aaron to collect them and hammer them out and attach them to the altar because they were holy. This was a very vivid response from God to the spirit of rebellion.

It would be nice to say that everyone else in the congregation now understood, but that was not the case. Israel didn't seem to learn anything from this experience, because the very next day, they rebelled against Moses and Aaron. The cloud of God's presence and glory descended on the Tabernacle. This should have gotten their attention, but they kept on rebelling. It is like the spirit of stupid comes over people who are caught up in a spirit of rebellion. This time, God only told Moses and Aaron to move away from the people. The people had their chance, but didn't accept the Lord or His anointed servants.

## OPPORTUNITY TO CONSIDER THE
## CHARACTER OF MOSES

Moses knew that something really bad was about to happen. So, he told Aaron to fill his censor, get the fire from the altar, and take it to the congregation for their atonement. Aaron literally took up a stance between death and life to save the people. Aaron courageously did what he was asked to do and stepped into the middle of God's wrath to make atonement for the very people who had risen up against him and against Moses. But on that day, 14,700 died before Aaron could make atonement and stop the plague. I want you to understand that rebellion is very serious business with the Lord.

Remember, this is not some old story that has no relevance for today. The message and lessons from Korah's rebellion are for the church age. In other words this lesson is for this moment in time. In the next to the last book of the New Testament, Jesus' brother, Jude, wrote:

*"Woe to them! For they have gone in the way of Cain, have run greedily in the error of Balaam for profit, and perished in the rebellion of Korah."* (Jude 1:11)

These are not just Old Testament stories and lessons. There is also a New Testament lesson for God's people. I want you to know and understand that this is serious business. God does not like a rebellious spirit. He does not bless a rebellion and He does not bless the rebels. We need to purge these tendencies from ourselves and our churches. Heed the words of the Holy Spirit in the book of Hebrews! Paul tells us that some people who had been flippant about communion and misused it had actually died. Death as a judgment on rebellion is New Testament theology. Some people say that it was like that in the Old Testament, but Jesus changed all that. They believe that Jesus is meek and mild and is a pushover for the church. This simply is not true. Remember He is coming back to rule with a rod of iron. If you think Jesus would never use death to punish rebellion, just look at Revelation 2:20-23. This is why we have the warning from the Holy Spirit in Hebrews, chapter 3.

> *"Therefore, as the Holy Spirit says: "Today, if you will hear His voice, Do not harden your hearts as in the rebellion, in the day of trial in the wilderness, where your fathers tested Me, tried Me, and saw My works forty years. Therefore I was angry with that generation, and said, 'They always go astray in their heart, and they have not known My ways.' So I swore in My wrath, 'They shall not enter My rest.'"* (Hebrews 3:7-11)

The Bible gives us another good example of God's judgment on rebellion. We looked at this briefly in an earlier lesson. However, it has a direct application here as well. King Uzziah was a great king. He did many good things to bless the Lord and the people. He was highly intelligent and ruled well. He had the heart of an engineer and personally developed new and more powerful weapons of war. The Bible tells us that he was right with God as long as Zechariah was alive. He accepted Zechariah's mentoring, and kept himself pure and focused on God. But in his later years, after Zechariah died, he became very prideful.

> *"But when he was strong his heart was lifted up, to his destruction, for he transgressed against the Lord his God by entering the temple of the Lord to burn incense on the altar of incense."* (2 Chronicles 26:16)

He made the same mistake that Korah and the 250 notable men made in the wilderness wandering. He came in with a censor to burn incense before the Lord. He decided he was good enough and powerful enough to step into their anointing.

Why did he need the priests, if he was just as holy as they were? When the priests tried to stop him, he was enraged and released his fury on them. Doesn't this sound familiar, and shouldn't we expect the same results?

> *"So Azariah the priest went in after him, and with him were eighty priests of the Lord—valiant men. And they withstood King Uzziah, and said to him, "It is not for you, Uzziah, to burn incense to the Lord, but for the priests, the sons of Aaron, who are consecrated to burn incense. Get out of the sanctuary, for you have tres- passed! You shall have no honor from the Lord God." Then Uzziah became furious; and he had a censer in his hand to burn incense. And while he was angry with the priests, leprosy broke out on his forehead, before the priests in the house of the Lord, beside the incense altar."* (2 Chronicles 26:17-20)

King Uzziah rebelled against the priesthood, and tried to step into their anointing. In his pride, he believed that as king he could do anything he wanted to do. That day, he decided to do priestly duties himself, but what a terrible outcome for this good king. Leprosy broke out on his face, and he was kicked out of the temple. And the next thing we read about him is:

> *"So Uzziah rested with his fathers, and they buried him with his fathers in the field of burial which belonged to the kings, for they said, "He is a leper." Then Jotham his son reigned in his place."* (2 Chronicles 26:23)

We must never forget how serious rebellion is in the church. We have other examples in scripture. Remember King Saul who did the same thing as Korah and king Uzziah. Samuel told him to wait until he arrived to make the sacrifice before the battle. But, Saul became impatient and offered it up himself before Samuel arrived. In his pride, he stepped into Samuel's anointing and suffered the consequences. He too was punished severely for trying to step into someone else's anointing. And all of Israel suffered when many of them died in battle that day because of Saul's rebellion. There are always consequences to rebellion, and they affect our families, our fellow church workers, and those close to us.

Have you ever wondered how many people have died early due to rebellion? Perhaps some people in your church have died early for this same reason. It is not popular to preach about these spirits, but considering the consequences I believe it is essential for those who would shepherd the people. We are reminded of this over and over in scripture. Listen to the words of Jeremiah:

> *"Therefore thus says the Lord: 'Behold, I will cast you from the face of the earth. This year you shall die, because you have taught rebellion against the Lord.'"*
> (Jeremiah 28:16)

God takes rebellion very seriously. Remember, in the ten commandments, God makes it clear that rebellious children will not live long in the land. God will remove rebellious people no matter how much good they may have done. No matter how smart they may be. When they rise up in pride and rebel against God or against those God has set apart and anointed for His work, the Lord will remove them.

Remember as you read the Bible, and see it over and over: God chooses; God calls; God anoints; and God removes! And, we need to let God do what God does, and we need to do what God calls us to do. May we never be among the ones who rise up in rebellion, because rebels don't live long. May we never come against the Lord's anointing or the Lord's anointed. It is so important to guard your heart against a spirit of rebellion.

## DON'T BECOME A PRESUMPTIOUS AND REBELLIOUS PERSON!

If you don't agree with a church or ministry and you can't resolve it through prayer, then you may have to leave. But, when you do decide to leave, don't rebel against God's anointed. Don't go against the pastor! Don't go against the board. Don't go against the elders and deacons. The fact that you don't agree doesn't remove God's anointing. Only God can do that. Don't gather a following and attack the anointing. Jesus told Paul that this is like kicking against a sharp stick. *"And he (Saul) said, "Who are You, Lord?" Then the Lord said, "I am Jesus, whom you are persecuting. It is hard for you to kick against the goads."* (Acts 9:5) Today is a good day to stop kicking against sharp sticks. Break off the rebellious spirit!

Don't try to gather people against God's chosen leaders. Listen to God's advice in the Word. Pharaoh rebelled against God and suffered the consequences.

"Therefore thus says the Lord: 'Behold, I will cast you from the face of the earth. This year you shall die, because you have taught rebellion against the Lord." (Exodus 14:13)

That is how God deals with rebellion. People in the early church rebelled against God and received this warning, *"Woe to them! For they have gone in the way of Cain, have run greedily in the error of Balaam for profit, and perished in the rebellion of Korah."* (Jude 1:11)

In a rebellion, always remember the power which God brings to the situation.

*"...and declared to be the Son of God with power according to the Spirit of holiness, by the resurrection from the dead."* - Romans 1:4

The Spirit of holiness comes with declarative power. The Spirit of holiness comes into your midst and declares who is right and who is wrong. When this occurs, you need to let the Spirit of truth take charge of your situation.

The Spirit of holiness comes with resurrection power, and what the world declares dead, is raised back to life. What the world calls foolish, the Spirit can show to be the wisdom of God. What the world declares as false, the Spirit can show as God's truth. And, the truth is that we need to submit to this Spirit, the Spirit of holiness.

When you're down, and people are disrespecting you, turn to the Spirit of Holiness and let Him raise you back up for service. Just fall on your face and let God raise you back up, because what you need to remember is that you are one of those the Lord has called forth, set apart, and made holy. Remember, the real meaning of the word translated as church is the called forth — those set apart for God's purpose and plan — those anointed by God to accomplish His will. You are at your best when You are operating in your own calling. When you operate in your own anointing, you do our best work. Then, when are you at your worst? You are at your worst when you try to step into another person's anointing.

Always remember that God does not bless those who are in rebellion. God has a winning plan. It is written down in a divine Op Order — our Bibles. Those who follow God's plan are blessed, favored, and successful. Those who follow God's plan are the wise and they will walk in the fullness of the blessing.

*"A highway shall be there, and a road, and it shall be called the Highway of Holiness. The unclean shall not pass over it, But it shall be for others. Whoever walks the road, although a fool, Shall not go astray."* (Isaiah 35:8)

You can't go wrong staying on the Highway of Holiness. So, let the Spirit of holiness come to you and tell you what your role will be. Listen to the Spirit of holiness as He tells you, "This is your calling! This is your anointing! This is what I am going to bless you in, and when you do it, you will have my help! My power will be available to you. But, when you try to step into someone else's anointing or rebel against the anointing in another, I may have to remove you. I'll come first to chastise. If you listen and repent, I will restore you. But, if you persist in rebellion, I may have to remove you." It is important for all of us to know that God will remove people to insure that His plans work. This type of removal will eventually happen to persistently rebellious people. But, my prayer for you is that you will be obedient to His Spirit and do what He wants you to do.

## PRAYER TO RELEASE THE SPIRIT OF HOLINESS

Father God we give you thanks today. We thank you for sending the Spirit of holiness to set us apart for your work and to strengthen us as carriers of the kingdom in this world. We thank you for the resurrection power this Spirit brings to us, and all who walk in obedience to our Lord, Jesus Christ. We thank you for the Spirit of wisdom and revelation which gives us direction, wisdom, counsel, understanding, might, and the fear of the Lord! We thank you for the Spirit of truth who guides us in all truth and defends us against the spirit of falsehood.

Father God you bless us so much through these Spirits sent out by our Lord Jesus in order to strengthen us and build us up into the body of Christ. Lord, we want to submit to you, be obedient to you, to follow you, and to do whatever you call upon us to do. So, we ask for a special impartation on each person open to your spirit; especially for the young people in the body of Christ. We ask you to bless each one and lift them up in the strength and power of your Holy Spirit.

We ask you to give each faithful follower increased understanding, authority, and power to sharpen the clarity of their anointing and the strength to fulfill your will for their calling. We ask you to release favor and blessing over each anointed disciple to enable them to accomplish the purpose of your calling on their lives.

When the enemy sends a spirit of rebellion, give us the discernment to recognize it and the strength to stand against it. Give us a greater sense of the presence of the Spirit of holiness to drive out every rebellious spirit in our midst. May we be faithful to our calling and pleasing in your sight, Father God. Amen and Amen!

## NOTES

# LESSON 4

# "THE SPIRIT OF LIFE"

Ⅰt was late in the afternoon when cooler air began to moderate the hot Texas sun in San Antonio. We had gathered between the Army Medical Command Headquarters and the Army medical school to say farewell to an era and to acknowledge a powerful legacy of service. I was participating in the ceremony to dedicate a retired MEDIVAC helicopter in memory of those teams who had rescued thousands of wounded service members. The Huey helicopter had been the workhorse of the ground warfare in Vietnam. Any time a Huey shows up today, you will see the eyes of every veteran fill with tears as memories flood into their conscious minds. Now, this Huey, a mainstay of the past, had been retired from service. It was an emotional moment as we gathered to dedicate it in memory of the brave men and women who repeatedly flew into harm's way to rescue the wounded.

A man walked up beside me and began to talk as the official ceremony was being conducted. Someone was reading the comments from the Surgeon General of the Army along with other official decrees. I was prepared to give a prayer of dedication and recognition of those who had served at such great risk to their on welfare. At first, I was a little annoyed that the man was talking during the ceremony. But as I listened, his story flooded out as tears ran down his cheeks. He said, "I am alive today because of a helicopter like this one. When the helicopter arrived the enemy fire was too heavy to land safely. The commander waved him off, but that brave crew would not pull back to safety. They landed near me under extremely hostile fire. When they loaded me on the helicopter, one of them actually apologized to me for the danger their takeoff would put me into. I was near death when I arrived at the field hospital, but the crew had stopped the bleeding and bandaged my wounds. I later heard the surgical team say that if I had arrived five minutes later, I would not have made it. By their heroic efforts, they had gotten me to the field hospital just in time. I owe my life to those who came for me at the risk of their own lives in the heat of the battle. Where do they find people like that? They were amazing. When I recovered I tried to find them to thank them, but was never able to locate them. When I heard about the service today, I just had to be here to remember them and express my gratitude to those unknown and unsung heroes."

I cannot remember one word of the official decrees or any of the cleverly crafted comments from those who spoke at that ceremony. I cannot remember one word that I prayed that day. But, I will never forget the impassioned words of this very grateful survivor.

Life and death meet face to face on the battlefield like no other place on this earth. Each moment provides an opportunity for a bullet, bomb, or piece of shrapnel to change life into death. Combat soldiers are intensely aware of the danger and confident in the evacuation systems and the medical teams who stand ready to take them quickly to safety when they are wounded. Life is never more precious than when you become aware that death is close at hand. Training, preparation, and preservation are the cornerstones of the service which conducts these life saving missions.

These meetings between the forces of life and death also occur in spiritual warfare. Those who would be warriors must prepare for these moments, and be confident that they will be taken out of battle when they are wounded and trust that they will be made whole again in the grace of God.

Welcome to the fourth lesson of spiritual boot camp! I hope and pray that you are becoming more and more ready for warfare as a result of this training.

Our Commander in Chief (CINC), 7-Star General Jesus Christ, has sent us a message concerning our preparations for war.

> *"Or suppose a king is about to go to war against another king. Will he not first sit down and consider whether he is able with ten thousand men to oppose the one coming against him with twenty thousand? If he is not able, he will send a delegation while the other is still a long way off and will ask for terms of peace."* (Luke 14:31-32, NIV)

It is very important that we continually remind ourselves that we are at war, because our enemy has already declared war against us and is attacking relentlessly. Moment by moment and day by day, our enemy is on the offensive. He has made his objectives very clear. He wants to totally annihilate each and every one of us. That is his objective, but it is not the last word in this matter. We have another Word from our CINC: Remember how Jesus described the intent of the enemy:

> *"The thief does not come except to steal, and to kill, and to destroy. I have come that they may have life, and that they may have it more abundantly."* (John 10:10)

By this teaching of Jesus, we know that our enemy's objective is to steal, kill and destroy. With this knowledge of the enemy's intent, we become painfully aware that this is a matter of life and death! We must be alert and ready! To survive, we must learn how to wage spiritual warfare.

As we have learned in previous lessons, we need to learn basic tactics and how to defend ourselves. We must know our weapons and learn how to use them skillfully. We must train and qualify on the spiritual weapons of warfare. We must not only know our own weapons, but we must also become familiar with the weapons of the enemy. We must learn specific survival skills needed in the life threatening environment of battle. We need to know first aid, so that we can bind up the wounded and restore them to fighting capability. We must learn the proper wear of our protective armor.

When we study the enemy's tactics and capabilities, there are critical elements that we must know and understand. We need to know how the enemy operates, in order to properly prepare our defenses against his offensive actions. We need to learn how to get off the defensive and gain the initiative so that we can take the battle to him. When we take the battle to him, we have the element of surprise working for us. It is time for a major counter offensive. If we are going to succeed at taking the battle to the enemy, we need to learn this basic combat skills.

We have also learned that we must develop skills at staying alert to ensure that we maintain security in our areas of operation. We clearly understand that we must stay on our guard against enemy attacks. We must not let the enemy get inside our perimeter where he can seriously damage our group. And, we know that we must not go to sleep when it is our turn to be on guard duty! We need to know how to establish and maintain security in order to deny the enemy the opportunity to surprise us.

We must always remember that we are not in this alone. God has deployed some of His most powerful resources to help us in the battle. We always have these friendly forces operating on our behalf. John describes these powerful spiritual forces in the fifth chapter of Revelation.

> *"And I looked, and behold, in the midst of the throne and of the four living creatures, and in the midst of the elders, stood a Lamb as though it had been slain, having seven horns and seven eyes, which are the seven Spirits of God sent out into all the earth."* (Revelation 5:6)

These seven spirits have been sent out to help us and also to fight for us. In other words, God sent the Holy Spirit to give us the strength and resources to stand and to overcome. Through the power of these seven Spirits, we become more than conquerors. To properly work with these forces, we must begin by valuing highly what God has entrusted to us.

> *"Guard the good deposit that was entrusted to you— guard it with the help of the Holy Spirit who lives in us."* (2 Timothy 1:14, NIV)

God will provide the power you need to accomplish His purpose. Remember how Jesus told the disciples to go to Jerusalem and wait for power.

> *"But you shall receive power when the Holy Spirit has come upon you; and you shall be witnesses to Me in Jerusalem, and in all Judea and Samaria, and to the end of the earth."* (Acts 1:8)

The purpose of the seven Spirits is to bring God's power to bear on the enemy and to give us the victory. We must step out of our comfort zones and enter the battle if we want to participate in the victory celebration. Then and only then will we be able to witness to the nations.

So far, we've looked at three (3) of these seven Spirits of God. We looked at the Spirit of wisdom and revelation (Spirit of prophesy). Who comes against it? (the spirit of Jezebel) Then, we looked at the Spirit of Truth. Who comes against it? (Balaam - the spirit of falsehood). finally, we looked at the Spirit of Holiness. Who comes against it? (Korah - the spirit of rebellion)

## BEFORE GOING INTO BATTLE, A COMMANDER MAKES A PLAN

When this plan is published, it is called an **OPERATIONS ORDER**. An operations order has five parts. The operations order gives you a clear understanding of the **SITUATION**. It clearly states the **MISSION** and describes the steps in the **EXECUTION** of the plan. It provides details of the **SERVICE AND SUPPORT** available to you, and the plan for maintaining **COMMAND AND SIGNAL** during the operation. In this lesson, we are going to look more closely at the first part of the plan: the situation.

The Situation has three (3) parts. One of the most important parts of the Operations Order is to evaluate friendly forces. You know that the best way to wage war is to form an alliance with other nations in order to magnify or multiply your fighting strength. You need to do this in spiritual warfare as well. Instead of churches acting independently, they need to come together, because in unity they can bring greater combat power to bear on the enemy. This means that you need to know before the battle begins if you have other friendly forces. You need to know who they are, what their strength and capabilities look like, and when they will be deployed.

After evaluating the friendly forces, you need to make an evaluation of the Enemy Forces. You need to have the answers to some basic questions. What does the enemy have for his fighting strength? How many soldiers does he have, and how well have they been trained? What weapons does he have, and how many are available at the time of battle? Weapons superiority is a great advantage on the battlefield.

The third part of the **SITUATION** is represented by the acrostic **OCAKO**. First the letter, "**O**" stands for "**O**bservation and fields of fire." You want to be in a position where you can see clearly and assign specific lanes for each element to engage the enemy. You establish fields of fire to bring maximum power on the enemy while reducing the likelihood of firing at one another. For the individual soldier, you often put two sticks in the ground: one on the left and one on the right to define the field of fire for that person. It is always to your advantage if you can establish positions on the high ground to give you greater areas of visibility.

The second letter, "**C**" is for "**C**over and concealment." Cover means that you have something between you and the enemy which protects you from small arms fire. Concealment prevents the enemy from seeing you and any movement you may make. The important question is: Can you position yourself so that the enemy has a limited ability to see and engage your forces?

The third letter "**A**" stands for "**A**venues of approach." Does the terrain limit the way you can approach the enemy? If there are avenues which provide more cover and concealment, you may want to travel that way. Another question relates to the limitations on the enemy's approach to your position? If there are clear avenues for the enemy to travel, you can concentrate your fire on those areas. But, you must remember that the enemy is doing the same evaluation. He will also concentrate fire on the best avenue of your approach.

A fourth concern is represented by the letter "**K**" which stands for "**K**ey terrain." Are their terrain features which can give you or your enemy an advantage during your operations? Knowing these key terrain features allows you to plan your movements as well as estimating the path any enemy forces will have to take when assaulting your position. Steep mountains, rocky valleys, lakes, rivers, and open areas are all key terrain features to consider in your estimate.

The final letter "**O**" stands for "**Obstacles.**" Are there natural or manmade obstacles to your movement or the enemy's movement which may limit your flexibility and reduce your chances of success?

In the book of Numbers, God begins to take command of Israel as His Army. In Chapter 13, God commanded Moses to send spies into the "promised land" before they moved in to engage the enemy. Did God need this information? No! God already knew the answers to all the questions. What God was doing at that time was providing a strategy for gathering the same kind of information we have been discussing. After God told Moses to send the spies, Moses gave the spies instructions on what to look for in their analysis. These instructions closely follow the steps in a modern day analysis of the situation.

It is important to keep the above information clearly in mind as you go into the next topic. At first, the new topic may seem like something completely different. But, I hope to clearly demonstrate the connectivity for you.

I would like to point to a key concept in scripture. In the Bible there is a concept which is referred to over and over. It is a reference to a "flow."

*"There is a river whose streams shall make glad the city of God, The holy place of the tabernacle of the Most High. God is in the midst of her, she shall not be moved; God shall help her, just at the break of dawn."* (Psalm 46:4-5)

Notice that there is a river which has streams, and there is a flow in it. What we understand in the natural can help us understand spiritual realities. When you are in an outpouring of the Holy Spirit, you can actually feel the flow of the Spirit in the same way you can feel the flow in a stream. With the spiritual gift of discernment you can actually tangibly feel the flow. Just ask anyone who has participated in a great outpouring of the seven Spirits on a group of believers. Jesus attempted to explain this to Nicodemus. Jesus was telling Nicodemus that if he was having difficulty understanding physical things, he was not going to be able get the teaching on the new birth. Jesus said,

*"Jesus answered, "Most assuredly, I say to you, unless one is born of water and the Spirit, he cannot enter the kingdom of God. That which is born of the flesh is flesh, and that which is born of the Spirit is spirit. Do not marvel that I said to you, 'You must be born again.' The wind blows where it wishes, and you hear the sound of it, but cannot tell where it comes from and where it goes. So is everyone who is born of the Spirit."* (John 3:5-8)

As Jesus said, the Spirit in born again people flows like the wind. You can't see where it comes from and you don't know where it is going. But, you can feel the flow of the wind. In the same way, when you are around Spirit filled people you can feel the flow. When you worship intently, you can feel the movement of the Spirit and you recognize that there is a flow. John also speaks about a flow which is coming from God's throne.

*"And he showed me a pure river of water of life, clear as crystal, proceeding from the throne of God and of the Lamb. In the middle of its street, and on either side of the river, was the tree of life, which bore twelve fruits, each tree yielding its fruit every month. The leaves of the tree were for the healing of the nations."* (Revelation 22:1-2)

John says that the flow is *"the river of the water of life."* This means that a spiritual reality is being described here. Basically, John is saying that life is flowing out from God and the Lamb just like water flows in a river. This life force of God, flows out to every living thing in the world. It is the spiritual force which sustains all life in our world.

*"He who believes in Me, as the Scripture has said, out of his heart will flow rivers of living water. But this He spoke concerning the Spirit, whom those believing in Him would receive; for the Holy Spirit was not yet given, because Jesus was not yet glorified."* (John 7:38-39)

Jesus makes the tie between this flow and a spiritual reality very clear in this passage. He didn't suggest that actual water would be flowing out of our hearts. That would be very strange. Jesus said that this flow was the Spirit which all believers were to receive after He had been glorified. It is important to note how much time Jesus spent teaching this idea. The time Jesus put into this teaching makes it clear how very significant it is for us. I believe that Jesus is pointing to a critically important reality: We should be able to actually feel this flow of the Spirit in those who possess it and release it?

This concept is tied to the release of the seven spirits. Now, with this concept of the flow in mind, let's look again at our basic text for this training.

*"And I looked, and behold, in the midst of the throne and of the four living creatures, and in the midst of the elders, stood a Lamb as though it had been slain, having seven horns and seven eyes, which are the seven Spirits of God sent out into all the earth."* (Revelation 5:6)

Think of these seven spirits being sent out as a flow from the throne of God. Jesus sends this flow out to us so that the power of God is available in our lives and work. Jesus pushed the point of the flow one step further in John 6:63, *"It is the Spirit who gives life; the flesh profits nothing. The words that I speak to you are spirit, and they are life."* It is this concept of "life" which makes it even more clear that Jesus is speaking about a spiritual reality which is sent forth to enliven our physical bodies. Jesus was telling us that the Life of God flows into us and through us as a work of the seven Spirits of God.

## ONE OF THE SEVEN SPIRITS IS THE SPIRIT OF LIFE

*"For the law of **the Spirit of life** in Christ Jesus has made me free from the law of sin and death."* (Romans 8:2)

This life is *"ZOE"* life! It is the very life of God given to believers. The life of God is like the flow of a river. It flows out from God into us, and then through us into the world. There should be a flow of the Spirit of life in every believer. In every circumstance you face, there should be a flow of life. The flow is to move through you into the atmosphere around you. It is a law. The Spirit of life then sets you free from the spirit of sin and death.

*"Inasmuch then as the children have partaken of flesh and blood, He Himself likewise shared in the same, that through death He might destroy him who had the power of death, that is, the devil, and release those who through fear of death were all their lifetime subject to bondage."* (Hebrews 2:14-15)

The writer of Hebrews makes it clear that sin and death are part of the domain of the enemy. These two things have kept us in bondage all our lives. We have been set free from the power of death by the flow of life which comes from God through Jesus Christ. Have you experienced that flow of life which Jesus sends out through the Spirit of life? When you see this flow moving in great revivals and in today's outpourings, it is like the life force of God (through the Spirit of life) breaks out in a group of people. And it breaks through whatever is happening in the lives of the people. In the midst of whatever gloom and doom people may be experiencing, the Spirit of life just breaks through and banishes the curses, death, and dying in the lives of the people.

When you are in an outbreak like that, you experience a surge of the Spirit of God moving in you as if you are being born again at a higher level of existence than you have ever known. And, you watch with joy as others catch that same Spirit of life and go through the same kind of transition you are experiencing. When that surge of life comes, it can be overpowering and you may be unable to stand any longer. Sometimes, it hits you so hard that it knocks you to the floor and seems to pin you down. It is fun to watch someone come in with a sour attitude as if covered with the spirit of death and doubt. Then the next thing you know, they are on the floor being filled with the Spirit of life. When they are able to stand again, their entire countenance has changed and you can celebrate the new life with them.

I love those outpourings and the experience of the flow of the Spirit of life. Wherever I hear of it breaking out, I do my best to get there and experience it anew. I love to be recharged with the Spirit of life and carry that flow with me when I leave.

Over and over, I have seen that in the midst of all this flow of life something happens and the outpourings literally die out. As you study the great revival movements of the past, you see that it happens over and over. Even while you are watching these things happen, you know that it just isn't right. This flow of life should be unstoppable, and you wonder, "What happened?" How could this happen to people who have seen the glory? How could it happen among a people who have been in the flow of the river of life? How can such a powerful revival suddenly be brought to a complete halt?

## THE ENEMY ALWAYS STRIKES AGAINST THE SPIRIT OF LIFE

The enemy always strikes against those who are experiencing the Spirit of life. He moves in with a surprise attack and does whatever it takes to block the flow of life. He will come against those who are leading the movement and he will come against anyone being empowered by it. That is who the enemy is and that is what he does. Remember his purpose is to steal, to kill, and to destroy. To get a better understanding of the principality he brings against the Spirit of life, study the book of Jude.

> *"But these speak evil of whatever they do not know; and whatever they know naturally, like brute beasts, in these things they corrupt themselves. Woe to them! For they have gone in the way of Cain, have run greedily in the error of Balaam for profit, and perished in the rebellion of Korah."* (Jude 1-10-11)

Notice that these invading spirits breach our security again and come into the group. The enemy is seeking to find weak individuals through whom he can launch his attack. Jude says these people are like brute beasts. In other words they are living fleshly lives rather than moving in the spirit. And, they willingly allow themselves to be used against the group. Armed with this knowledge, you can accurately evaluate the risks in advance. You can identify people who are at risk to be used by the enemy to do his dirty work on the inside of your group. Jude gives us the clue in verse 16. "These are grumblers, complainers, walking according to their own lusts; and they mouth great swelling *words,* flattering people to gain advantage." I have seen this happen over and over. It always comes through those who constantly grumble and complain and have no reservations about taking advantage of others.

In verse 19, Jude gives another key to identifying those in our group who are at risk. "These are sensual persons, who cause divisions, not having the Spirit." The enemy seeks people who by reason of a character defect cause divisions in any group they join. They love to get others caught up in their complaints and they attempt to turn them to grumbling. Listen to Jesus' take on this. "'*Stop grumbling among yourselves,*' Jesus answered." (John 6:43, NIV) That's pretty clear. Jude explains that these people don't have the Spirit (Holy Spirit), and they attack those who do have the Spirit of life.

Jude is very clear that the enemy brings the spirit of Cain (spirit of murder; also known as the spirit of death). This is not Cain. He died centuries ago. However, we know that this spirit which controlled Cain is still alive, because it was operating in the New Testament church. These New Testament churches are mentioned, because they are representative of the body of Christ throughout the church age (now). To understand this spirit we look back at the first murder recorded in the Bible.

> *"Now Cain talked with Abel his brother; and it came to pass, when they were in the field, that Cain rose up against Abel his brother and killed him. Then the Lord said to Cain, "Where is Abel your brother?" He said, "I do not know. Am I my brother's keeper?" And He said, "What have you done? The voice of your brother's blood cries out to Me from the ground."* (Genesis 4:8-10)

Abel had no idea what was about to happen. His brother invited him to go out to the field. That sounds like fun, but Cain's intent was to kill him. That is what the enemy does, and that is what he wants to do to you. He wants to kill you. Like

Cain, he will invite you to a place or event which sounds like fun and then, he will attempt to destroy you. We don't like to think that we really have an enemy who wants to kill us, but it is a fact which we must live with every day. Why do so many bad things happen? It is because there is an enemy who craftily works through others to kill innocent people; especially those who are flowing with the Spirit of life.

Most people think it won't happen to them. They are certain they would never actually murder anyone. And, they feel confident that this spirit will never get control over them. You may feel very innocent because you haven't actually murdered anyone. Yet, you may commit spiritual murder almost every day with poison words. You can literally kill people with the words from your mouth. Many people use their tongues as powerful and destructive weapons to assassinate someone's character, destroy their ability to work with a group, and/or steal their good name and professional reputation. Words can hurt and words can kill. How are you using your words? You need to be alert and watch to make sure that the enemy cannot use you this way. You need to pay close attention to Paul's warning to the Galatians.

> *"If you keep on biting and devouring each other, watch out or you will be destroyed by each other."* (Galatians 5:15, NIV)

Biting and devouring each other will destroy your group. Have you heard people say, "I chewed him/her out!" And, that is literally what they did. They were biting and devouring someone, and they are very proud of it. They were trying to beat them down; break them down; and kill their spirit. A church can be destroyed by biting and devouring. This is what Paul was saying to the Galatians who were under the influence of the spirit of Cain. It is a deadly thing people do with their tongues. Notice that when you fall for this trick of the enemy, you are brought down with the others. When the group fails, each member fails. You wind up eating the fruit of your own words.

*"Death and life are in the power of the tongue, And those who love it will eat its fruit."* (Proverbs 18:21)

When you consider how much damage you can do with your tongue, you can see why gossip, slander, and lies are literally hated by God. We are told in scripture that God abhors this kind of behavior.

*"These six things the LORD hates, Yes, seven are an abomination to Him: A proud look, A lying tongue, Hands that shed innocent blood, A heart that devises wicked plans, Feet that are swift in running to evil, A false witness who speaks lies, And one who sows discord among brethren."* (Proverbs 6:16-19)

Why does God abhor these things? He hates them, because they are a direct attack on His Spirit of life. They are carried out by people who have allowed the enemy more influence over their spirits than God's Holy Spirit. They have fallen for his deception and have started to attack the group from within. They become traitors to the cause of Jesus Christ, and bring great damage to the body and it's witness to the world. Our best witness to the world is the love we show for one another. Our worst witness to the world is this biting and devouring of one another. Who would want to be a part of a group like this?

When the Spirit of life is at work in the church, the spirit of Cain will always be released by the enemy, and it will move in quickly to launch an attack! I can confidently guarantee you that this will happen, because I have seen it over and over. When a church is coming alive, moving, and growing, the spirit of Cain will always come in. Then you see members of the group who begin to literally bite and devour one another. By doing this, they will block the movement of their own church group.

In Psalm 10, the palmist describes the behavior of the wicked who move in the spirit of Cain. Remember that Psalm 10 was probably part of Psalm 9 where David is dealing with the depth of wickedness which leads to murder. We know that these two psalms are connected because they have been written and arranged to form an acrostic. The first letter of each section is part of the Hebrew alphabet, and you must put the two psalms together to complete the alphabet. Here we see more of the character of one who is under the control of the spirit of Cain.

> *"His mouth is full of cursing and deceit and oppression; Under his tongue is trouble and iniquity. He sits in the lurking places of the villages; In the secret places he murders the innocent; His eyes are secretly fixed on the helpless. He lies in wait secretly, as a lion in his den; He lies in wait to catch the poor; He catches the poor when he draws him into his net."* (Psalm 10:7-9)

The spirit of Cain is a very destructive spirit. His goal is to bring death — to literally eat up and destroy God's people. He uses the tasty morsels of gossip to lead people into an enemy ambush. You may have seen some of this in yourself when your heard some gossip about someone you don't really like. The words are like tasty little morsels. Maybe you heard something about a political candidate you didn't like, and the words were like tasty little morsels. If you keep taking in these tasty little morsels, watch out, because it won't be long before you are operating in the full power of the spirit of Cain. Then you will find yourself ambushing and attacking others. However, look closely at what has happened to you. You have just stepped into an enemy ambush. We have to be smarter than that! We have to be better prepared than that. We must stop participating in these things.

When people give in and allow themselves to be controlled by this vicious spirit, their words literally become deadly. Listening to them, you think they will only be happy when someone is dead. They begin to speak more and more hate and destruction into the lives of other people. This spirit will rip a church apart, and that is exactly what it is seeking to do. It will destroy the fellowship in the body of Christ, and that is another of its goals. It wants to stop the flow of the Spirit of life in the body of Christ. The higher the body count in these battles the greater the victory for the enemy, and the greater the defeat for the church. This is why Paul cautioned the Roman church: *"Bless those who persecute you; bless and do not curse."* (Romans 12:14)

You have to do better than this! You have to be better than this. You must learn the enemy's tactics and prepare your defenses well in advance of the actual battle. You must learn to immediately identify the spirit of Cain and stand against it in unity with others in the church. You must be vigilant, because it comes when you let down your guard. It happens when you are spiritually asleep and not standing guard.

Remember the penalty for someone who falls asleep on guard duty during a time of war. This is so serious that most military organizations use the death penalty to deal with it. This is very serious business. We have been playing at church for too long, and failing to take seriously the warnings of the Lord. God is gracious and forgiving, but we can push him too far. Jesus gave a parable about knowing when the enemy will attack.

*"Another parable He put forth to them, saying: "The kingdom of heaven is like a man who sowed good seed in his field; but while men slept, his enemy came and sowed tares among the wheat and went his way. But*

*when the grain had sprouted and produced a crop, then the tares also appeared. So the servants of the owner came and said to him, 'Sir, did you not sow good seed in your field? How then does it have tares?' He said to them, 'An enemy has done this.' The servants said to him, 'Do you want us then to go and gather them up?'"*
(Matthew 13:24-28)

Remember, one of the worst things in war is for the enemy to get inside your perimeter. Military units learn to fight back to back, firing at the enemy in all directions, but never firing at each other. But, when the enemy is inside the camp, you begin to hit your fellow soldiers. This is tragic, and it happens over and over. You may think, "This couldn't happen to us, and it certainly couldn't happen to me." The people who don't believe it could happen to them are the most vulnerable. People who say this are the first ones the enemy comes to, because he knows he can use that arrogant attitude and pride to deceive them. We see over and over the people who deny it the most are the ones who are used first. Watch out then, and keep on the alert. We are at war, and the enemy wants inside the camp.

God gives us watchmen on the wall and guards to keep an eye out for enemy movement. The watchmen and guards must always be alert and ready. When the enemy gets into the camp, many people wonder, "Why doesn't God just remove them?" Why doesn't God just come in, shut their mouths, and remove them? Why doesn't God do that? Well God did take care of it. He gave the job to us, and told us over and over how important it is to remain alert. When we are asleep on watch, it is not God's fault.

In addition to letting us be responsible for our area of assignment, there are other important reasons why God doesn't remove people from the body of Christ right away. He has other plans, and the KEY is found in this parable.

*"But he said, 'No, lest while you gather up the tares you also uproot the wheat with them. Let both grow together until the harvest, and at the time of harvest I will say to the reapers, First gather together the tares and bind them in bundles to burn them, but gather the wheat into my barn.'"* (Matthew 13:29-30)

God doesn't want someone to be lost because another person is being removed. People are interconnected. If someone is removed for cause, others can be taken out with them. When some people see others being removed, they get offended and will leave the church over the offense. The enemy likes to use offense to block them from getting established in another group. They may blame the entire body of Christ because they were hurt in one place. God doesn't want them to be lost. Another reason is that God doesn't want to pull a weed which is almost ready to be converted to wheat. The Spirit of life may be ready to come into that weed and totally transform it into a planting of the Lord. God sees the things we can't see. God knows the future and the outcome for each of us. In His wisdom and grace, he does not uproot people out of season.

## THIS OFTEN HAPPENS IN THE AREA OF WORSHIP

I want you to notice how often this happens in the area of styles of worship. People are very sensitive about how they worship and many are easily offended by how others express themselves in worship. I have listened to people make great accusation about a revival because of the way people respond. Do you remember the "laughing revival?" I have met people who are still offended by it. They point to a lack of dignity and make accusations about the silliness of so much laughter. Don't you just love it when some of these people get hit with the laughter and are unable to stop.

Some people seem to believe that certain songs and certain tunes are more sacred and holy than others. They are offended when songs they don't know or don't like are used in worship. People get upset about how the collections are taken, and the amount of time spent talking about it. Some people get upset when others come under the power of the Spirit and fall down. Still others get offended when they hear someone pray in the Spirit. There seems to be a great deal of smugness and self-pride tied to all of these accusations. Remember the first attack by the spirit of Cain:

*"And in the process of time it came to pass that Cain brought an offering of the fruit of the ground to the Lord. Abel also brought of the firstborn of his flock and of their fat. And the Lord respected Abel and his offering, but He did not respect Cain and his offering. And Cain was very angry, and his countenance fell. So the Lord said to Cain, "Why are you angry? And why has your countenance fallen? If you do well, will you not be accepted? And if you do not do well, sin lies at the door. And its desire is for you, but you should rule over it."* (Genesis 4:3-7)

At first it may be difficult to see why Cain's offering is a problem. But notice that he just brought some fruit. It doesn't say that he brought the first fruits or the best fruits. He just brought some fruit. When someone doesn't see their offering as special, they don't connect much weight to its importance. However, God is serious about it. He made a covenant to bless us in accordance with our offerings. When we offer little, we limit His response. This doesn't please our God of abundance. Cain was limiting God's blessing in his own life and God was telling him that he could do better.

Able was blessed because he brought the first born and the best portions to God. Able was serious about making an offering and it pleased the Lord. The Lord looked on Able with favor. Instead of learning a lesson from this, Cain became jealous of Able. He couldn't see that a simple change in his behavior could bring God's favor. All he could see was that his brother received what he thought belonged to him. In a jealous rage, he decided to kill his brother to remove the competition. The result was that both Cain and Abel were taken out of the game.

The enemy knows how to manipulate people in the area of worship. This is an area of particular expertise on the part of the enemy. As a former worship leader in heaven, he knows the temptations which can come into a person and lead them into pride and eventually into destruction. And, because he knows how to create division in this area, we see all these battles over styles of worship today. People even go so far as to accuse each other of heresy. This is an attempt to murder one another with hate filled words. They seem to believe that if you can destroy the credibility of an opponent, you can win arguments. But, this is a deception, because there is no real victory here. No one wins this battle. In a mudslinging contest everyone gets dirty.

Everyone loses except the enemy. While everyone is beaten and battered, he just sits on the sidelines laughing at them and celebrating his success. When you side with the enemy, you will always lose. He has already lost the battle and he wants to take as many as possible into defeat with him.

Do you know who was the first person in the Bible to be cursed? It was Cain. This is recorded in Genesis chapter 4.

> *"And He said, "What have you done? The voice of your brother's blood cries out to Me from the ground. So now you are cursed from the earth, which has opened its mouth to receive your brother's blood from your hand. When you till the ground, it shall no longer yield its strength to you. A fugitive and a vagabond you shall be on the earth." (Genesis 4:10-12)*

only a curse without a cause will not alight

Take note of this verse. If you want to be cursed by God, start operating in the spirit of Cain. Adam and Eve fell, but they were not cursed. The ground was cursed. The serpent was cursed. Adam and Eve were admonished, but not cursed. Cain was the first human to come under a curse.

Cain limited his own options so that he only had two choices. He could change his worship or kill his brother. He did not choose wisely. God gave him another option, but he didn't consider it. He chose to kill the one who worshipped in a way that pleased God. How could anyone think that this would please God? How could anyone in his wildest imagination think this would bring God's favor? Yet, people do the same thing every day. They viciously attack, bite, and devour others in order to appear better to God. They have somehow become blinded to the fact that this will never please God. It never has, and it never will bring His favor.

The spirit of Cain continues to deceive people the same way. I want you to know that Satan has very few new tactics. The reason for that is, the old ones still work very well. When we get focused on ourselves and begin to take offense at things others do, we are easy prey. We become targets set up for the spirit of Cain. Satan's greatest weapon is getting us to take "offense," resulting is us attacking each other. You see it when husbands and wives get offended, fights begin, and marriages end.

The family is the strongest unit in God's sovereign plan to surround people with love. Satan wants to destroy the family to break the power of God's love and grace. Children get offended by their parents, and get into rebellion or run away breaking the solidarity of the family. Church members get offended and strike out at others. When people get offended, their mouths begin to spit out hateful words and spiritual curses. This is tragic because of the damage it does to all of us. The spirit of Cain takes over, and breaks the bonds within the family of God. This is the point of our greatest vulnerability and we must learn to defend the territory against all enemies, foreign and domestic. That is our oath of office as soldiers of God. That is our code, and that is the stand we must take.

## THE ENEMY HAS DECLARED WAR
## AGAINST THE SAINTS

At this point, you may be saying, "Well, I just want peace. I'm not going to fight! If I don't fight, the war is over!" If this is your position, I have some bad news for you. It doesn't matter what you say! It doesn't matter what you want! It doesn't matter what you decide! When the enemy declares war, you ARE AT WAR whether you like it or not! In wartime, you are either part of the solution or part of the problem. There is no in between position in spiritual warfare.

The enemy's big plan is to get believers to think like that, and just stand on the sidelines. Whether you are on the sidelines or the frontlines, the enemy has the same goal for you. It doesn't matter where you stand. He is coming for you.

When I was stationed at Fort Monmouth, N.J., I had this wonderful relationship with an elderly Rabbi. I really loved that man. He was one of the most gentle and kind men I have ever met. He would come to visit me often, and it was always the highlight of my day. I truly enjoyed being with Rabbi Mordecai Daina. One day that sweet, kind, and gentle man came in outraged and ready to go to war. He wanted to call the troops together and he had already called the Jewish War Veterans to enlist them in the fight. This was a side of him I had never seen before. He was so furious and he was literally up in arms. So, I asked, "Rabbi Daina, what's going on? Why are you so upset? He replied, "Didn't you hear! New York has banned nativity scenes on all government property and in all government buildings!"

This was surprising because, Rabbi Daina was an Orthodox Rabbi, and yet he was ready to fight against taking nativity sets off government property. To understand this, you have to know that Rabbi Daina grew up in Poland. He personally experienced the Nazi's coming into Poland and taking Jewish people to the concentration camps. When he fled the persecution, he connected with a US Army unit and served as an auxiliary rabbi. He was one of the first to enter one of those concentration camps to see the horrors of what had been done to his people, his neighbors, and his family. So, he explained to me what this had taught him. He said, "One thing we learned in Poland. If you sit by today while the enemy takes your neighbor away, he will come for you tomorrow." Then he said, "If we sit by while the government takes away your nativity sets, tomorrow they will come for us."

You see there is an enemy, and he is coming for us. If we sit by while he takes our neighbors, we can be sure that he will come for us tomorrow. When you see the spirit of Cain and do nothing, you are in agreement with the enemy. We have to rise up and join in the battle. We must rise up, and release more of the Spirit of life. The answer to the spirit of Cain has always been to release more of the Spirit of life. We are not going out to buy guns so we can have a shootout. But there are powerful spiritual weapons available to us, and one of the most powerful weapons is the Spirit of life.

We must stop biting and devouring each other. We must stop listening to gossip. We must stop spreading gossip and the hateful words of the enemy. When someone starts talking about someone else, we must learn to say, "I don't want to hear it. I don't want to talk about someone unless they are here to participate in the discussion. I don't want to hear it!" This biting and devouring has got to stop. Just say, "No!" We must refuse to participate!

How can it be that this message was sent to the church almost 2,000 years ago, and we are still struggling with it? We've got to get smarter than that. We've got to get better than that. And, we must learn the weapons of warfare. We need to understand both the enemy's weapons and the Lord's weapons of warfare. The Spirit of life is a powerful weapon, and I want you to understand how powerful it is through the story of the two witnesses for God in Revelation 11. These two witness were very powerful and withstood everything the Antichrist could throw at them for 1,260 days. Then the Lord allowed them to be killed. The world was jubilant at the seeming victory of the Antichrist. The people were so perverse that they actually exchange gifts like at Christmas time to celebrate the deaths of these two individuals. Their bodies were left in the streets for three and one half days for people to look at them and mock them. But, God turned this seeming defeat into a glorious victory.

> *"And after three days and an half **the Spirit of life** from God entered into them, and they stood upon their feet; and great fear fell upon them which saw them."* (Revelation 11:11, KJV)

Look at the response of the enemy. Great fear fell upon all of them. It fell on everyone in the enemy camp; on every one of Satan's warriors; on every demon and devil of hell; on every witch and warlock; and everyone standing with the Antichrist. Great fear fell on them. The Spirit of life is a powerful weapon of war that strikes terror into the heart of every enemy of Jesus Christ. Demons and devils tremble in the presence of this Spirit. Many of us have grown up unaware that this Spirit is available. We have not understood how to use it or how to release it in a timely manner.

This is the time! This is the season to enlist in the army of the living God. This is the time for us to take back the offensive, and take back the territory stolen by the enemy. We don't simply get into a defensive posture and attempt to set up boundaries. We don't accept the idea that there are things which belong to him on his side of the wire, and try to barely hold on to the things on our side. The enemy loves to be in a war of attrition where he can take us out one by one and claim our territory for himself. We must deny him this opportunity. It all belongs to God, and we have been put in charge. We need to rise up and take back everything that belongs to the Lord. We need to take the battle to him, bind him up, and cast him out. We need to declare that we will not give up any more territory. We will not give up one more soul. We are taking the initiative, and hitting him deep in his own territory. We will not be content until we bring it all back into the kingdom of God. Amen?

This is spiritual boot camp. As you learn these things, I want you to know that the enemy will come for you. You must learn about the enemy. You must understand his weapons and his tactics. You need to know his strength, capabilities, and weaknesses. Did you catch that last part. He has weaknesses, and we must learn to exploit his weaknesses. And, never forget that God is on your side. Our awesome, unstoppable, all powerful God has sent the Spirit of life to bring absolute victory to us.

We must seize the offensive, and put the element of surprise on our side. It is time to pick up this powerful weapon (the Spirit of life) and destroy the works of the devil. Know this: the enemy will come for you whether you study and prepare or not. It is much better to be prepared, watching, and waiting. Take heart! Do not be afraid! Be courageous and strong, because the Spirit of life is with you in the battle.

Remember: the Spirit of Life has resurrection power. It is the awesome power of life — God's life force (Zoe). We need to release it into every situation and every conflict. We must always stand with Jesus in the flow of life. John cautions us:

> *"For this is the message that you heard from the beginning, that we should love one another, not as Cain who was of the wicked one and murdered his brother. And why did he murder him? Because his works were evil and his brother's righteous." (1 John 3:11-12)*

Remember that the enemy is terrified of the Spirit of life, because he knows that when it comes into its fullness his time is up. There is nothing left for him except the lake of fire. Every demonic spirit and every principality of the enemy knows this and trembles. Release it and take your unwavering stand for the Lord. And when you have done everything to stand, keep on standing in the power of the Spirit of life.

## PRAYER FOR RELEASING THE SPIRIT OF LIFE

Lord God, we come before you in the powerful name of Jesus Christ. And with the authority He has given us over scorpions, snakes, and all the power of the enemy — Today, we decree that we bind the spirit of Cain! We bind the spirit of murder! We bind that spirit that comes out of our mouths with words of death and destruction! We bind that biting and devouring spirit in the name of Jesus. We bind it up and command it in the name of Jesus to depart from us and go into the pit of hell and stay there for all eternity!

Today, Lord, we want to release the Spirit of life and release that flow of living water. We want to release rivers of living water from our hearts as part of that ultimate flow of life coming from you, Father God. May this flow of life proceed from us today and always in the mighty name of Jesus. Father God, we are here! We are available! Enlist us in your spiritual Special Forces. Father God, we submit ourselves to you as we resist the devil in the glorious name of Yeshua ha Messiach! Amen and Amen!

## NOTES

# LESSON 5

# "THE SPIRIT OF SONSHIP"

M any soldiers who have served in the Army for a few
years will say, "I joined the Army and found a home." In
a military unit, people become very close. They work together,
play together, live together and fight together. A special bond
of trust begins to form with any group which goes into harm's
way to accomplish a mission for their country, their home, and
their family. You know that your life may depend on the person
or persons next to you in battle, and it is essential that you be
able to depend on them. It is equally important for them to be
able to count on you. Many soldiers who face terrifying situations say they were able to get through it because they didn't
want to let their friends down. In one sense, joining the army
is like being adopted into a family. You develop a common
identity and you are committed to common goals. A sense of
belonging is one of the most basic needs of the human spirit.
We have been uniquely created to bond together and form a
sense of family.

I believe this is one reason why we so readily accept an
understanding of ourselves as members of the family of God.
We are called to a common purpose and we help each other
to achieve our common goals and meet our common needs.
We have a common enemy who is trying to steal our bless-

ings, kill our dreams, and destroy our effectiveness in ministry. We need to trust one another and be certain that we can count on each other when the battle begins. As in a military unit, we need to have this bond of trust with each other in order to survive in spiritual warfare. Soldiers who do not complete the bonding process normally do not last long in a military unit or in a church.

One day while serving as the chaplain at Brooke Army Medical Center, I was making my rounds of the clinics and common areas. In the lobby, I saw a retired chaplain I had served with many years ago. He was in the hospital with his wife, and they both seemed out of place. I asked them if they had an appointment or if they needed assistance. His wife said, "No! He just needs to be around soldiers once in a while. When the Army Times newspaper arrives at the house, he says, 'Here's my hometown newspaper!'" Long after retirement, most career soldiers still feel this sense of belonging in their military family.

Welcome to the fifth lesson of spiritual boot-camp which will deal with this basic need for belonging and how the enemy uses these needs to strike out against us in one of our areas of greatest sensitivity. I want to begin by reviewing our primary text for this training.

*"And I looked, and behold, in the midst of the throne and of the four living creatures, and in the midst of the elders, stood a Lamb as though it had been slain, having seven horns and seven eyes, which are the seven Spirits of God sent out into all the earth."* (Revelation 5:6)

As we begin this lesson, I want to remind you that we are at war with a determined and deadly adversary. To win this war, we need to bond together in our common defense. That is one of the reasons why it is so important to remain prepared and alert. Our spiritual family members are counting on us to help keep them safe. Failing to prepare, prepares you to fail! It is not easy to grasp the reality of warfare. No rational person wants to be engaged in war.

After almost 30 years on active duty as an army chaplain, I have never met a commander or general officer who wanted to go to war. War is a terrible thing, and the toll it takes is very high. In movies and on television, you see people playing generals who are craving the opportunity to go to war for their own career goals or for other distorted personal reasons. However, I never met even one single person with any combat experience who wanted to go to war and be caught up in those horrors again. It simply doesn't happen that way. If you don't want to be at war, good! You are a rational person. However, we don't have any choice when an enemy declares war and persists in attacking us at every opportunity. If we must be at war, we should learn to conduct our part well to minimize losses and maximize success. To accomplish this, we must be ready, alert, and vigilant.

Getting soldiers to stay awake and remain in a state of high alert is a constant challenge. I was stationed for a number of years at a post which was part of the Communications and Electronics Command. We were all required to complete annual training on security and espionage. In the training we were made aware that there were KGB agents working in every club, bar, and restaurant in the area. They were constantly seeking young men and women with financial and personal problems which could be exploited. They were able to persuade several to become spies against their own country. Most of those caught committing these crimes would tell the same story. They thought they could just do a little and make enough money to get out of trouble. To their surprise and shock, once they sold a few little secrets, the KGB owned their souls and there was no way out. Threats of exposure were used to frighten them into doing more. The only way out was to be caught, arrested, and sent to prison for life. You see, agents of the enemy don't care what happens to you. They don't care if you get caught and punished. They don't care if your life is ruined and your reputation is destroyed. They have diplomatic immunity and in the worst case scenario they will have to move. They will turn you in themselves if they get tired of you or you stop being useful for their purposes.

This is the kind of bondage the enemy wants to place on us. The devil wants to own your soul and control you destiny. He doesn't care about you. He will use you and then discard you. He will turn you in and laugh at you during your arrest, trial, and punishment. He has no love or loyalty and there are always others he can use. If you give in to his tactics and begin to do his dirty work, you immediately become a disposable asset. He will turn on you quickly and do what his nature inclines him to do. He will steal your hopes and dreams. He will kill you destiny, and he will destroy everything you have ever done or hope to do for the Lord. The only way to stay free is to remain vigilant and loyal to the God you serve.

Jesus knew this struggle over loyalty very well. He knew the pain of having one of those in His inner circle sell out to the devil and betray Him. Like the victims of espionage today, Judas' only way out was death. In addition to what Judas did, Jesus' closest disciples fell asleep on duty at one of the most critical points in His life. They slept while the enemy moved in for the kill. Then each and every one of them fled to save his own life and left Him at the mercy of a merciless enemy. In his gospel account, Mark records the incident this way:

*"Then He came and found them sleeping, and said to Peter, "Simon, are you sleeping? Could you not watch one hour? Watch and pray, lest you enter into temptation. The spirit indeed is willing, but the flesh is weak."* (Mark 14:37-38)

You can sense the pain in Jesus' voice as He confronts the sleeping disciples. The comment he made to them is an eternal truth, and it's the same today. "The spirit is willing, but the body is weak." We're called to go against our human nature with all its frailties. How can you do what you are being asked to do? How can you remain awake and alert when you are so fatigued from the battle? On the other hand, how can you remain alert and awake when there seems to be no threat? Either situation (the intense fatigue from war or the relaxed sense of peace) puts us at risk of losing our readiness posture and falling prey to an enemy attack.

Paul advised his spiritual son Timothy, "Be diligent to present yourself approved to God, a worker who does not need to be ashamed, rightly dividing the word of truth." (2 Timothy 2:15) You must be diligent in order to present yourself approved to God. You must study your SMART book (Soldier's Manual and Readiness Training, which is your BIBLE) and store the Word of God in your hearts. You are called by the Lord to be a workmen who is not ashamed, because you have studied to rightly divide the word of truth. The Word of God is the Sword of the Spirit, and it is your only offensive weapon for warfare. As with warfare in the natural, you must learn and practice all your military skills for spiritual warfare. And, you must learn to know, understand, and use your weapons of spiritual warfare which are the seven Spirits of God.

So far, we have looked at four (4) of the seven Spirits of God and examined which enemy spirits come against us when these Spirits are working in our lives and in our churches.

First, we looked at the Spirit of wisdom and revelation also known as the Spirit of prophecy. When an anointing to operate in the prophetic or an increase in this anointing comes to an individual or church, the enemy will respond and send a strong spirit against us. Who comes against it? The enemy sends the spirit of Jezebel against the prophetic anointing. This spirit attempts to take control over the prophet, the pastor, and ultimately the entire church. This wicked spirit must be cast out of the church to avoid the judgment of Jesus coming upon the ministry.

Next, we studied the Spirit of truth. We know from other scriptures that this is a direct manifestation of the Holy Spirit. With the Spirit of truth comes great enlightenment about the will and purpose of God, and the enemy sends another principality against it. Who comes against it? The spirit of Balaam or more commonly known as the spirit of falsehood comes to hinder the flow of the Spirit of truth. To counter attack, we release even more truth to break the power of the enemy's lies.

Then, we studied the Spirit of Holiness which comes to support and empower the five-fold ministry in the church and especially the apostolic anointing. God sets people apart for ministry to train and equip the saints to accomplish His purpose. When this begins to flow powerfully in the church the enemy sends a principality to hinder it. Who comes against it? The spirit of Korah, also known as the spirit of rebellion is sent to block the work of the Holy Spirit in the church.

The fourth spirit we studied was the Spirit of Life. When we see a great move of the Spirit to bring new birth to sinners and new life to tired saints and weakened churches, the enemy tries to destroy this work. Who comes against it? The spirit of Cain or the spirit of death/murder is sent to counter this Spirit. This may appear as an attempt to destroy the reputation, effectiveness or ministry of any or all the members of the church. We must heed the warning given by Paul to stop biting and devouring one another.

The fifth Spirit of God we are looking at in these lessons is the "Spirit of sonship." This Spirit is also known as the "Spirit of adoption."

*"For you did not receive a spirit that makes you a slave again to fear, but you received __the Spirit of sonship__. And by him we cry, "Abba, Father." The Spirit himself*

*testifies with our spirit that we are God's children. Now if we are children, then we are heirs—heirs of God and co–heirs with Christ, if indeed we share in his sufferings in order that we may also share in his glory."* (Romans 8:15-17)

## KINGDOM BUILDING REESTABLISHES RELATIONSHIPS

Without the "Spirit of sonship," you can't really call Him Abba, Father. Your relationship with the Father is established by this Spirit. It is this Spirit which sets you free from slavery or as the NKJV says "the spirit of bondage again to fear." This Spirit has set you free from slavery to sin and death and connected you to the life giving flow of God. When you are separated and distanced from the Father, your relationships can be restored by this Spirit. When you experience alienation, separation, and isolation from the Father, this is the Spirit which restores those relationships. If you feel distanced from the Lord, you need to call on this Spirit to restore you to fellowship with Him. You can easily see why it is so critically important for you to understand this Spirit, and for you to allow yourself to be reconnected with the Lord. It is by this Spirit that you are built up and made fit for service.

*"And because you are sons, God has sent forth the Spirit of His Son into your hearts, crying out, 'Abba, Father!' Therefore you are no longer a slave but a son, and if a son, then an heir of God through Christ."* (Galatians 4:6-7)

Without the "Spirit of sonship," you don't have an inheritance, because your inheritance is based on your position in the family. This is the Spirit which bonds us together as family, and our spiritual inheritance is for those of us who are His children. If we are not His children; if we are not sons of God, we have no inheritance from Him. Without the Spirit of Adoption, you will not have an inheritance on earth, and without it you will not have an inheritance in heaven.

Without the "Spirit of sonship," we are still slaves to fear, slaves to sin, and slaves to death. Without this gift of God, there is plenty to fear. But, thank God, He sent Jesus to make it possible for us to receive this awesome gift of adoption into the family of Father God. Thank God He didn't leave us in spiritual poverty! Thank God He didn't leave us in sin and death! Thank God He didn't leave us as little alien children running away from Him! Instead, He sent Jesus as the author and finisher of our faith. He sent Jesus to bring us home and reunite us with our eternal family. He sent Jesus with the awesome and powerful "Spirit of sonship" to say, "You are my brothers!"

I want to make a comment about gender at this point. I don't believe gender matters to the Lord, and in His sense of humor, He calls us to become sons so that we can be the bride of Christ. The NIV uses the phrase "Spirit of sonship" as the best translation of this passage. Others use the phrase "Spirit of adoption" in order to be more inclusive. Either way, this and every other gift from God is inclusive of men and women. I back up this claim with Paul's teaching in the third chapter of Galatians.

*"For you are all sons of God through faith in Christ Jesus. For as many of you as were baptized into Christ have put on Christ. There is neither Jew nor Greek, there is neither slave nor free, there is neither male nor female; for you are all one in Christ Jesus. And if you are Christ's, then you are Abraham's seed, and heirs according to the promise."* (Galatians 3:26-29)

It is the Spirit of sonship which makes all these things possible for us. This powerful Spirit makes all these wonderful gifts of the Lord available to us through this most awesome gift of adoption. As family members, all of God's spiritual gifts are available to us. I believe this is why women receive the Spirit of sonship. It is to insure that they receive their full inheritance. In the time of the New Testament, daughters received a much smaller portion. Now as sons, they are entitled to a full share of the inheritance. The Spirit of adoption is so critically important to our relationship with Jesus and Father God, and yet, so many of us don't really understand it. Remember, you are either a son or a slave. There is no in between. You either have the Spirit of sonship or you have the spirit of bondage again to fear. You choose, but choose wisely.

*"But when the fullness of the time had come, God sent forth His Son, born of a woman, born under the law, to redeem those who were under the law, that we might receive the adoption as sons. And because you are sons, God has sent forth the Spirit of His Son into your hearts, crying out, "Abba, Father!" Therefore you are no longer a slave but a son, and if a son, then an heir of God through Christ."* (Galatians 4:4-7)

We have been redeemed from the law of sin and death. We have been set free from the spirit of fear; especially the bondage of fear which leads again to sin and death. Through this Spirit, we know that Father God will not abandon us to the will and intent of the enemy. Remember Jesus' promise in John 14:18 (NIV), *"I will not leave you as orphans; I will come to you."* We have been redeemed into a saving relationship with the Father. You are redeemed from certain things, but you are also redeemed into other things.

When this Spirit of sonship brings the reality of your adoption into your spirit, you no longer have to pray to an unreachable and distant God. You can now talk in prayer with your loving Father. It may be hard to grasp, but it is legal for you to say, Abba, Daddy, Papa, or whatever familiar word you may want to use for this loving Father with whom you have a relationship of pure love. Now, you are authorized to go to God and say something like, "Daddy, I love you!" If you have ever been a father or mother, you know how good it feels when your child comes to you with outstretched arms and says, "Daddy, I love you!" or "Mommy, I love you." Jesus wants you to know that your Father in heaven likes that too. He loves for His children to come to Him just to hug and be hugged, and to hear them say, "Daddy, I love you!"

The reason God went to such extremes to bring us home is because, He loves us and loves to hear us express our love for Him. That's why He asked His Firstborn Son to pay such an awful price. That's why He asked Jesus, "Are you willing to go to their world and suffer a death which will pay the penalty for every sinful thing they have ever done? Are you willing to go and break every last bit of shame off of them? Are you willing to go and pay such an awesome price to bring them home? Are you willing to die on the cross to make it happen?" And Jesus said, "Yes! I'm willing! I will go!"

That's why when Jesus lived among us and discovered what pain felt like; how much it hurts; He went to the garden and said, "Daddy, is there any other way. Pain really hurts. But, if there is no other way, I will still do it, because they are that important. I'm willing to go through it so we can be together as a family forever!" This Spirit of sonship is very powerful and changes our destiny from slave to son. This Spirit of sonship is so very important for us, and that's why the enemy will not just ignore it.

## WHEN THE SPIRIT OF SONSHIP COMES, THE ENEMY RESPONDS

When this Spirit of sonship comes into you, your family, or your church and you start to really experience this closeness and fellowship with God, the enemy will come. When people start reconnecting with God, and the power of His love begins to flow more and more, other people are drawn to Him by the power of this Spirit. This is a huge threat to the enemy and his plans. Because of this, he will come against you, your family, and your church. To postpone his own fate, he is determined to hinder the flow of this Spirit of God. He knows that when this begins to happen, his days are incredibly short. When the bride begins to get ready, divorces herself from Baal, and embraces the Spirit of sonship significant things begin to shift in the spirit realm. When the bride is ready, Christ will return, defeat the enemy, and dwell with the saints forever. No wonder Satan fights so hard to block this Spirit.

Satan knows that when this happens he only has a short time — a little less than seven years. He will then be thrown into the pit for a thousand years. He knows how bad this pit is, because it was his creation. It is so nasty and so bad that demons beg not to be sent there. It is so bad that they would rather be completely dead than spend any time there. And the only break Satan will have from this terrible place is a short trip to the lake of fire where he will burn forever and ever. Some authors have made it sound like this is a place where the devil will rule and reign, but that is not the picture in Scripture. He will go there to be bound and punished forever and ever. He will not be causing your suffering, he will screaming in pain at his own. That is why he wants to delay it as long as possible, and we need to deny him this option. We need to embrace the Spirit of sonship and hurry the time of his end.

Know this with certainty: If you receive and hold to this Spirit of sonship, all the enemy's works will be destroyed in your life. When you receive and cling to this Spirit of sonship, Jesus succeeds and Satan fails. The victory over sin and death is totally with Jesus, and there is nothing left for Satan, and he knows it.

Because Satan knows this, he sends an awful spirit against the Spirit of sonship. He sends a wicked and nasty spirit against this Spirit of God. He sends the spirit of slavery or bondage which leads back to fear, sin, and death. Paul assures his spiritual son Timothy, *"For God has not given us a spirit of fear, but of power and of love and of a sound mind."* (2 Timothy 1:7) God did not send the spirit of fear or the spirit of bondage. These two nasty spirits were sent out by the enemy to block the work of the Spirit of sonship. Because this spirit leads people back into bondage to the enemy, it can also be called the spirit of slavery to sin and death. Through fear and bondage, this spirit deceives people into believing that God has abandoned them. People are deceived, because God has not abandoned them. He will never leave you nor forsake you. However through the spirit of bondage to fear and death, the enemy has tricked some people into abandoning God. God makes this clear in His message given through Ezekiel.

> *"Therefore speak to them, and say to them, 'Thus says the Lord God: "Everyone of the house of Israel who sets up his idols in his heart, and puts before him what causes him to stumble into iniquity, and then comes to the prophet, I the Lord will answer him who comes, according to the multitude of his idols, that I may seize the house of Israel by their heart, because they are all estranged from Me by their idols."'* (Ezekiel 14:4-5)

When people are deceived by the enemy into following his false ways, they estrange themselves from God. Instead of recognizing this, repenting, and dealing with it, they blame it on God. This is what the enemy wants you to do. He raises questions about your relationship with the Father by asking if you are a slave or a son. He wants you to question whether the Father really loves you. He wants you to question whether God will really take care of you when the hard times come.

He wants you to question whether God has really forgiven you and removed your sin. Don't forget what he tried to do to Jesus when he repeatedly asked, "If you really are the son of God...?" This is such a nasty spirit, and when it comes we need to remember what Paul said to the Romans:

> *"For you **did not receive the spirit of bondage again to fear**, but you received the Spirit of adoption by whom we cry out, "Abba, Father."* (Romans 8:15)

From the garden to the wilderness of temptation, he has done the same thing over and over. In the garden, he asked Eve, "Did God really say that to you?" She started to wonder about God's motives. Maybe, he wanted to deny them something which was good for them. Maybe he was withholding the best gifts. Then she added to what God said, and distorted the truth of His word. When she did this, the serpent took away from what God said. With all these questions, Eve finally separated herself from faith in God. But instead of freedom, knowledge and power, she was made a slave to sin and death. That's what the enemy does. By tempting you into doubt and disobedience, he gets you to separate yourself from God and put yourself in bondage to him.

There are many Biblical accounts of the enemy working to separate God from His children. Those with a powerful anointing are especially at risk, We see this spirit of bondage to fear clearly at work in the relationship between King Saul and David.

> *was this spirit of false prophecy?*
>
> *"And it happened on the next day that the distressing spirit from God came upon Saul, and he prophesied inside the house. So David played music with his hand, as at other times; but there was a spear in Saul's hand. And Saul cast the spear, for he said, "I will pin David to the wall!" But David escaped his presence*

*twice. Now Saul was afraid of David, because the Lord was with him, but had departed from Saul. Therefore Saul removed him from his presence, and made him his captain over a thousand; and he went out and came in before the people. And David behaved wisely in all his ways, and the Lord was with him. Therefore, when Saul saw that he behaved very wisely, he was afraid of him."*
(1 Samuel 18:10-15)

Because of his consistent disobedience, the Lord withdrew His favor from Saul, and Saul felt like God had abandoned him. Instead of becoming humble, repenting, seeking the Lord, and living right, he began to blame others. We see this same thing in people all the time. They don't take personal responsibility for their separation from God, but find someone else or something else to blame. In doing this, they separate themselves more and more from God. Have you heard that old question, "When you find yourself far from God, who moved?" In reality Saul had moved. He had abandoned his loyalty to God long before God withdrew His favor. Eventually God abandoned His hopes and plans for Saul.

When Saul saw that God's Spirit was with David, he became jealous and afraid. Saul's character defects and lack of discernment led him to go back into bondage to the spirit of fear. When he saw that God's Spirit was with David, he saw clearly that God had abandoned him. He knew that the greatest threat to the throne was the man on whom the Spirit of God rested. He feared what David might do to him, his descendents, and his heritage when God put him on the throne. On one occasion, Saul said to David:

*"And now I know indeed that you shall surely be king, and that the kingdom of Israel shall be established in your hand. Therefore swear now to me by the Lord that you will not cut off my descendants after me, and that*

*you will not destroy my name from my father's house."*
(1 Samuel 24:20-21)

This spirit of bondage to fear left Saul open to many other enemy spirits. The spirit of Cain came upon him, and he tried to kill David several times. The spirit of falsehood came upon him and he made up all kinds of false stories about David's loyalty. The spirit of rebellion came upon him and he followed his own way while abandoning God's way. Saul's fear grew stronger and stronger until he was enslaved by it. Every attempt to harm David failed, because God protected him.

David had received the Spirit of sonship, and remained strong and faithful in the worst of circumstances. He did not let an offense lead him into a murderous spirit. He remained faithful to God and refused to do any harm to the Lord's anointed leader. After being anointed by Samuel to rule over Israel, he waited patiently until God's timing was right. Through the Spirit of sonship, David knew that God was with him and would keep His promises.

In this account of the fall of Saul, we see how the spirit of bondage to fear takes people on a downward spiral until they are beyond help. The Bible is full of stories of people abandoning God and His statues. This always has disastrous effects. We see it in Adam and Eve when they abandoned their trust in God in the Garden. Judas didn't get what he wanted and he then abandoned and betrayed Jesus. Because of his bondage to fear, Peter abandoned Jesus during His toughest moments: the arrest, trial, and crucifixion. The Psalmist aptly describes all of these individuals:

*"Yet they tested and provoked the Most High God, And did not keep His testimonies, But turned back and acted unfaithfully like their fathers; They were turned aside like a deceitful bow."* (Psalm 78:56-57)

If you are going into battle, do you want to take a faulty bow with you? Would you like to pull on the string and just have it all fall apart in your hands? Understanding this, try to imagine how much the Lord wants us to become reliable, faithful, and dependable. Are we? As we reflect on this verse, it should lead all of us to do some soul searching. How much of this is in us? If we see it, how do we remove it? How do we repeatedly fall into this terrible pattern of fear leading to bondage?

As Jesus said, we need to be as wise as serpents and harmless as doves. We must remain alert at all times, and avoid enemy traps. Almost every time someone falls back into fear there is a spirit of offense behind it. Offense is the most effective tool used by the enemy to produce disloyalty and disobedience in members of the church. When Jesus was doing His ministry many people were offended by Him and missed the hour of their visitation. Jesus said, *"And blessed is he who is not offended because of Me."* (Luke 7:23) The Pharisees and citizens of His home town were offended by what he said and did. When Jesus gave a prophetic word about the Lord's Supper, many of his own disciples were offended and left Him. On that occasion He questioned the remaining disciples,

*"Then Jesus said to the twelve, "Do you also want to go away?" But Simon Peter answered Him, "Lord, to whom shall we go? You have the words of eternal life. Also we have come to believe and know that You are the Christ, the Son of the living God." (John 6:67-69)*

If people were offended and abandoned Jesus, we can be certain that people will be offended by you as well. You need to get over being surprised by the enemy's attacks. You know his tactics and you know his plan. Don't be surprise! Be ready! Readiness includes getting over being offended by others. Don't let the enemy deceive you and control you this way!

People are so easily offended over very small incidents. Someone may park in the place which they are accustomed to using or sit in the pew where they normally sit. Instead of just shrugging it off and taking another place. They become offended. For others it begins with a situation in which they believe they were unfairly treated. Perhaps a co-worker receives special recognition or gets promoted ahead of them. As they focus on the seeming unfairness of the situation, their feelings progress from jealousy to offense. If allowed to continue, these emotions progress to anger, disloyalty, fear, and rebellion. Before long they either quit their jobs or strike out at the ones whom they perceive to be favored. They have truly gone back into bondage to fear, sin, and death.

We also see this happening in families. Husbands or wives get offended and then begin to strike out by telling others about the terrible things their spouse has supposedly done. We see it happening between parents and children. Someone gets offended and then says terrible things about a friend, loved one or church leader. Others get offended and respond back often using stronger words of accusation and anger. Disloyalty begins to permeate all the relationships. You see it in churches when people think that the pastor offended them by something he/she said. When people begin to spread all the disloyal stories about one another it can get so ugly. It is a terrible thing to watch and realize that it is motivated by such an ugly spirit. Without realizing it, they are all being lead back in to bondage to fear, sin, and death.

People today are so disloyal and disobedient. You can talk to the employees in a store and they will voluntarily tell you all the terrible things about their boss or management. When you listen long enough, it almost always leads back to some minor offense. You see it at a national level when the news media, politicians, leaders, and teachers spew out so many accusations and twisted words to dishonor others. At times it seems like there is no allegiance or loyalty left in the world today. When this happens we know that the enemy has plundered us. He has stolen our innocence, virtue and trust. There is almost an epidemic level of dishonor today from overly sensitive people who are leaving a legacy of hostility, separation, and fear. When people lose trust in their leaders and supportive institutions, there is a sense that everyone feels abandoned by family, friends, communities, and God.

## HOW DO YOU DEAL WITH THIS
## SPIRIT OF BONDAGE?

There is a basic human need for love, acceptance, and favor. People need to know that they are loved and accepted by their family, their friends, their co-workers, and most of all by God. We were created by God with a huge need for love, and the purpose of this human need is to draw us to Him. In this country, during the cold war era, the communist party exploited this need to win converts. They set up organizations to specifically meet the needs for love, recognition, and acceptance. Tragically for those who fell prey to these recruiting techniques, these promised blessings were quickly removed as soon as they had people hooked. Then fear of disclosure and punishment led people into slavery to their new cruel taskmasters. Our enemy, the devil, uses the same tactics and techniques. He lures people into his web of deception by seemingly meeting their needs. But, as soon as they are hooked, everything shifts to fear and intimidation. Those who were once free are now forced back into bondage by fear.

God created us to need acceptance, so He could give it. God just loves to lavish acceptance, blessing, favor and love on His children. He made us to need it so He could have the joy of giving it. God has not withheld any of these blessings from us. On the contrary, God has done everything possible to bless us. Jesus is our living proof of God's loyalty and faithfulness toward us. Revelation 19:10, *"For the testimony of Jesus is the spirit of prophecy.*" You don't have to go searching for proof. Jesus is our proof! When we share testimonies of what God has done for us through Jesus, we are prophetically implanting an awareness of the love, favor, and acceptance God has given. Jesus sent the Spirit of sonship out into all the earth (Revelation 5:6) so that everyone could be drawn back into the family of God and out of their bondage to fear and death.

We are at war and the enemy wants to steal all these good things from you and then tempt you to blame God for the loss. He doesn't want you to have the blessings of the Lord. So, he tries to kill your hopes and dreams and rob you of your destiny and inheritance from the Lord.

The first step we must take in dealing with the spirit of bondage leading to fear is to examine ourselves. How strongly is this spirit working in us? Are we easily offended by others? Do we nurse an offense and help it to build in intensity? Do we strike out at those who seem to be blessed or favored? Do we let jealousy cloud our relationships with others? When we experience these things, do we feel distanced from God? Do we have feelings of being abandoned by God? Are we letting fear lead us back into bondage?

We cannot clearly see what is happening in others until we get ourselves free from bondage. If we feel the slightest sense of disloyalty toward others, we must take it to the Lord and ask for healing. We need to take it to the Lord quickly every time it occurs and allow the Holy Spirit to minister to our needs by releasing more of the Spirit of sonship into our hearts.

Our part of the warfare is to claim the adoption and sonship for ourselves and then to release it into others. Release the Spirit of sonship into every person and on every occasion when you see the spirit of bondage working to produce fear, and lead them back into bondage to sin and death. If you feel abandoned or see it in others, release the Spirit of sonship. This is our nuclear class weapon to destroy the work of the devil. This is the powerful weapon which can overcome fear and bondage.

Use it often and use it well. This Spirit will destroy the works of the devil when he tries to make you feel abandoned.

When you are tempted to be disloyal, remember Jesus' loyalty to the Father. He was so totally loyal that he was willing to die as an act of obedience. Jesus is our model. We are led by the Holy Spirit to be loyal and obedient sons and daughters just as our Lord Jesus was faithful to the will of the Father.

The Holy Spirit is the most powerful force on the face of the earth. Jesus didn't send the seven Spirits of God just to make a show. He didn't send them out to be mere window dressing. He didn't sent them out so He could say, "Look what I can do!" Jesus sent them out to be powerful weapons of spiritual warfare to fight with us and for us. Jesus released this awesome power in order to destroy the works of devil. This Spirit works every time. The Spirit of sonship has worked every time it has been released and it will always work in the future.

## ITS IMPORTANT TO SEE — WE MUST BE LED BY THE SPIRIT

*"For as many as are led by the Spirit of God, these are sons of God. For you did not receive the spirit of bondage again to fear, but you received the Spirit of adoption by whom we cry out, "Abba, Father." The Spirit Himself bears witness with our spirit that we are children of God, and if children, then heirs—heirs of God and joint heirs with Christ, if indeed we suffer with Him, that we may also be glorified together."* (Romans 8:14-17)

If you are not led by the Spirit of God, can you still be a son? It is important to consider this question very carefully. Look again at what the scripture says: "For as many as are led by the Spirit of God, these are sons of God." If you are not spirit led, you have not qualified to be a son of God. There has been much false teaching in this area by people who desire to make it easy for people to accept Jesus. These people have been very seeker sensitive, and they are sincerely trying to win people for Jesus. But, they are sincerely wrong in what they teach. We need to be honest with people. You must be led by the Holy Spirit to be a son of God. There is no shortcut to discipleship. If we fail to teach these truths, we are sending a generation of fighters into battle unarmed.

We see so clearly today that there is a big problem in the church because people are being led back into bondage by their oversensitive reactions. This is one of the main problems in the area of bondage to fear. People are being led by offenses rather than by the Spirit of God. People are being led by fear rather than the Spirit of God. Without the leadership of the Holy Spirit the distance between God and people continues to grow.

God has always been faithful to you and to all His children. If we continually confess God's faithfulness, we build it into our hearts. Say it now: "God has always been loyal to me!" Find someone else that you can confess this to. Say to them, "God has always been loyal to you!" We need to confess God's goodness all the time. Say it aloud to yourself now, "God has always been faithful to me!" Then find someone you can speak this promise into. Say to them, "God has always been faithful to you!" The more we confess His goodness, the more we will be built up in our most holy faith. The more we confess it over others, the more we both get built up in our faith. God is so good! He has been loyal to us even when we have not been loyal to Him. He has not abandoned us even when we have separated from Him. He has sent the Spirit of sonship to bring us back into relationship with Him and with one another. Thanks be to our God and Father! Amen?

Pause and think for a moment what you feel when you have to deal with someone who has been disloyal to you. Did it evoke love, compassion, patience, loyalty, and joy in you? When someone is disloyal to you, do you want to spend a lot of time with them? Do you enjoy their company and feel free to confide in them all your personal secrets? Do you feel like blessing them and telling other people about the good things you see in them? Most of us don't react this way. The human tendency is to find a way of getting even; we plot ways of giving them hurt for hurt. When we give in to this temptation, we just fall into the pit of hell. All of the good things God has placed in us begin to spoil and evaporate. We have to do better than that, but it is not easy. When we see ourselves honestly, we know how good God is, and we see that He continues to remain loyal to us even in our worst moments. Doesn't He deserve better from us?

> *"Nevertheless they flattered Him with their mouth, And they lied to Him with their tongue; For their heart was not steadfast with Him, Nor were they faithful in His covenant. But He, being full of compassion, forgave their iniquity, And did not destroy them. Yes, many a time He turned His anger away, And did not stir up all His wrath; For He remembered that they were but flesh, A breath that passes away and does not come again."*
> (Psalm 78:36-39)

We see this pattern in so many characters in the Bible. They are disloyal to God, yet God brings them back. God went back to Adam and Eve in the garden. He could have broken His relationship with them; abandoned them, and let them die alone. He could have responded by saying, "Look at that! After all that I did for them, they treated me with such contempt. I'll just abandon them and let the forces of nature wipe them out. Then, I will create some new ones. Maybe they will be better!" But, that's not what God did with Adam and Eve. He went to them and taught them the consequences of their actions and gave them an opportunity in new circumstances to be faithful to Him and their calling.

Peter was disloyal in the hour of Jesus' greatest need. You know that must have hurt Jesus very deeply even though He had prophesied it. Jesus could have written him off and he would have disappeared in the annuls of history with the reputation of being a disloyal friend and a loser. But, that's not how Jesus operates. Jesus took special care to welcome him back. Remember the message the angel gave the women. *"But go, tell His disciples—and Peter—that He is going before you into Galilee; there you will see Him, as He said to you."* (Mark 16:7) The angel didn't presume that Peter would feel included among the disciples. So, he gave a special word to include Peter. Jesus restored him and returned him to his destiny in the church.

David sinned greatly, but when he prayed a sincere prayer of repentance, God forgave him, and restored him. God could have just rejected him forever. He could have abandoned David in his sin and let that be the last chapter of his life. God didn't do that. He sent Nathan the prophet to him, and through that process restored him to his destiny and his calling. God is always good, and He is always willing to restore those who turn to Him.

Don't let some cheap, lying, treacherous spirit say anything other than that to you about God. Don't listen to him. Don't listen to the devil telling you about the Father. He lied about the Father in the Garden of Eden, and he has been lying ever since. He wants you to distrust God and distance yourself from Him. He wants you to abandon God and return to the bondage of fear and death. Don't listen to him! God has always been loyal to me. Say it again out loud: "God has always been loyal to me!" Say it over and over until it is stored in your heart. Say out Loud, "God will never let me down!" Say it over and over until it takes root in your heart so deeply that no demon or devil from hell can ever uproot it from your spirit.

When the enemy tries to lure you away from Father God, say, "No! I am going to stay close to Him, praise Him, worship Him, and stay loyal to Him all of my life!" Perhaps you can get to the place where you can say truthfully as Job did, *"Though He slay me, yet will I trust Him."* (Job 13:15)

Try this one. Say out loud, "I'm going to build myself up! I am going to trust God and rely on His faithfulness no matter what may come!" Then find someone you can build up with testimonies of God's goodness and faithfulness to you. God is always faithful, and He will not abandon you or let you down. Stay close to Him and He will stay close to you. Praise Him for His faithfulness, and in doing so, build yourself up in faith.

Don't let even the smallest disloyal thought or fear of bondage take hold of you. When you allow a small bit of that to work in you, it is like bait in the mouth of a fish. The devil will sink the hook into your jaw and reel you in. Remember: he wants to steal, kill and destroy. Don't let him lead you for even one moment. Covenant now to be loyal to the Father forever and ever. Covenant now to stay close to Him so that you can feel how close He is to you. Don't give the devil a foothold in your spirit. Reject it immediately. Call on the Spirit of sonship to come into your spirit right then. This is your most powerful weapon to avoid fear and the spirit of bondage. As you keep yourself free, you will see more and more clearly how to help others get free and stay free.

Would you pass a loyalty test today? This is something we had to do all the time in the military. To me those tests were painful. Periodically, we were commanded to go through training on security, espionage, and sabotage. We would be shown pictures and videos of those who had sold out their country and we would be required to listen to their stories. After the training, we had to go through a long form with many questions relating to various ways we may have intentionally or accidentally compromised our loyalty. There were long lists of groups and organizations known to practice espionage and sabotage against the United States of America. One by one, we would have to take an oath that we had never belonged to, worked with, or participated in meetings or activities of any of these groups. Perhaps we need training and testing like that in the church.

Today, we've had some of the training, and the test is very brief. There is only one question. Are you loyal and faithful to Father God, Jesus Christ and the Holy Spirit? If your answer is yes, hold on to it and never let it go. But, if your answer is no, make a fresh start today. You can be restored. Sincerely repent and seek God's forgiveness. He is always faithful and always just. He will forgive and restore.

Always remember what God has done for you. Give Him thanks and praise for what He has done or is doing for you. I prefer to err on the side of giving Him too much credit than not enough. So, I thank Him for everything that could be part of His favor. I am convinced that the more grateful you are, the more He gives. The more you acknowledge Him, the more He gives you to acknowledge. You know something about this if you have been a parent. You know the joy of giving to a grateful child. You will give what they need even if they are not grateful, but it is a joy when they express love and gratitude. This behavior will also make you willing to give more and more.

One of the most powerful ways to avoid disloyalty is to constantly give thanks and praise. When you see and acknowledge all the blessings from the Lord, you can't help but be drawn into a deeper relationship of trust and loyalty. It becomes a passion in your spirit to please Him and the Holy Spirit. When you live this lifestyle, the devil has no foothold in your life. When you constantly confess the goodness of God, you will not even be tempted to be disloyal to Him.

*"Blessed be the God and Father of our Lord Jesus Christ, who has blessed us with every spiritual blessing in the heavenly places in Christ, just as He chose us in Him before the foundation of the world, that we should*

*be holy and without blame before Him in love, having predestined us to adoption as sons by Jesus Christ to Himself, according to the good pleasure of His will, to the praise of the glory of His grace, by which He made us accepted in the Beloved."* (Ephesians 1:3-6)

Remember that the Lord has blessed you with every spiritual blessing. Think about that! Before the world began, God had already chosen to give you blessings and favor. He wants you to have everything that He has to give — every spiritual blessing. Meditate on that next part of this passage. He decided to adopt you as his sons through Jesus Christ before the world was created. That is a powerful thought, and when I think about these things, I want to shout and sing His praises. I want to give Him my total allegiance every day for the rest of my life on earth and in eternity.

Keep this in mind. He has not withheld any blessing from you. If you are even slightly tempted to complain that someone got something instead of you. Go back to this verse and confess it instead of the enemy's words which always accompany an offense. Father God has given you every spiritual blessing. When you are tempted to say: "Why is it that I have to carry all of these spiritual burdens, when everyone else seems to be free?" When that whining spirit comes into you, go back to this passage and confess that God has provided for every need and He has given every spiritual blessing to you. He has not withheld any spiritual blessing you need. You may have blocked the blessing, but He did not withhold it from you. Stay loyal to Him, and allow the blessing to flow to you and through you. *"And all these blessings shall come upon you and overtake you, because you obey the voice of the LORD your God:"* (Deuteronomy 28:2)

Long before you were born, God chose to adopt you. He chose to send the Spirit of sonship to confirm your relationship with Him. Stay loyal to Him always and in everything. If any other thought comes into you, go back to James 4:7 and declare it aloud, *"Therefore submit to God. Resist the devil and he will flee from you."* I promise you that if you will sincerely pray this when something comes on you, it cannot stay on you.

Use the weapons God has provided for you, and let the power of your confession drive the devil away. Begin to praise the Lord and the devil will lose interest. One of the things I like to do in an attack is to start confessing, "I am loyal to God! I love God! I praise God! I bless His holy name! And, my God has not withheld anything from me of the good things which I need! No spiritual blessing has been withheld from me! Praise be to the God and Father of our Lord Jesus Christ who made us sons, so that we can say, "Our Father!" We can cry out, Abba, Father! He is so good!" Use the Spirit of sonship, and avoid the spirit of bondage to fear.

Remember this powerful promise from Jesus, *"I will not leave you orphans; I will come to you."* (John 14:18) No one who follows Jesus will be an orphan again, nor will they be abandoned to go back into bondage to fear and death. In addition, Jesus promises to manifest Himself to those who love Him and keep His commandment

> *"He who has My commandments and keeps them, it is he who loves Me. And he who loves Me will be loved by My Father, and I will love him and manifest Myself to him."* (John 14:21)

As I prepared this lesson, the Lord told me to release impartation with this lesson. If you will extend your hands to receive it and pray this aloud, I believe that the impartation will come to you in power.

## PRAYER TO RELEASE THE SPIRIT OF SONSHIP

Father God, I release into my life and into the lives of all those around me that Spirit of sonship. Lord God, we have learned that every spiritual blessing comes with this Spirit. So, Father God, I release all seven of the Spirits. We break off any hindrance to the flow of the Spirits in our lives, we bind them up in the mighty name of Jesus, and decree that they depart now in Jesus' name. May the seven Spirits flow in and through each person who is open to being led by the Holy Spirit.

I release the seven spirits in my life and decree that I love you, worship you, praise you, and give my loyalty to you. I delight today that I can call you Daddy, and I pray, "Daddy, release the flow of your Spirit in my life right now. Jesus promised that the Holy Spirit would guide me in all truth, and I am placing a claim on that promise right now. In the power of these seven Spirits, send us out to release the flow of these spirits in the lives of those you have called us to reach in ministry. I raise my hands and receive it in the mighty name of Yeshua ha Messiach! Amen and Amen!

## ADDITIONAL SCRIPTURE REFERENCES TO BUILD YOUR FAITH

1 Timothy 4:1 (NIV), "The Spirit clearly says that in later times some will abandon the faith and follow deceiving spirits and things taught by demons."

Acts 2:26-27 (NIV), "Therefore my heart is glad and my tongue rejoices; my body also will live in hope, because you will not abandon me to the grave, nor will you let your Holy One see decay."

Nehemiah 9:31 (NIV), "But in your great mercy you did not put an end to them or abandon them, for you are a gracious and merciful God."

Deuteronomy 4:31 (NIV), "For the LORD your God is a merciful God; he will not abandon or destroy you or forget the covenant with your forefathers, which he confirmed to them by oath."

## NOTES

# LESSON 6

# "THE SPIRIT OF GRACE"

It is extremely rare to find a soldier who enjoys the first few weeks of basic training. During four years of service as a chaplain in a basic training unit, I can assure you that the most common feeling expressed by soldiers is hatred. They have left their entire support system back at home, and now have been merged with masses of new people. Their individuality seems to have been stripped away, and they are not allowed to make decisions for themselves. Many complain that they feel like they are in prison rather than in the army. When you have the opportunity to visit with them in this early phase of training, most will complain bitterly that the army is not good enough for them.

Over the next few weeks, they develop friendships, learn how to get their needs met, find ways to stay out of trouble, and sense that they are beginning to develop some very important skills. They begin to understand that they are not in this alone and success always depends on a group effort. A certain camaraderie and sense of pride begins to develop. And most begin to develop a sense of belonging.

As the sixth week begins, everything is focused on the testing phase which is coming up. And, usually for the first time, another type of questioning begins to emerge: "Am I good enough to be a soldier? Do, I know enough to pass the test? Can I meet the physical challenges?" As the time of final testing draws near, a sense of insecurity begins to surface in most of the trainees. This is good, because it pushes each soldier to study harder, practice longer, and focus more intensely on their individual and team skills. Up to this point, the drill sergeants have found it necessary to force them to read their SMART book. Now, they are looking for more time to study, practice, and prepare.

As you enter this sixth week of spiritual boot camp, I wonder if you are going through some of the same feelings. Have you learned the lessons well enough to handle the next enemy attack? Are you battle ready? Do you know how to use the weapons, wear the armor, and work as a team to be a good soldier for the Lord? Have you spent enough time in your SMART (BIBLE) book? Will you know what to say and what to do when you are face to face with the enemy?

In the sixth week of basic training you have to go back over everything you have learned to make sure that you are ready. You have to be willing and able to work as a team so that you can fight side by side with other spiritual warriors. So, let's do a quick review of where we are in this training.

So far, we've looked at five (5) of the seven Spirits of God. We've learned which enemy spirits come against us when the Spirits of God begin to flow. We've learned to examine ourselves and get free from all entanglements we may have with these spirits. We know which weapons to use.

1. Do you know who comes against you when the Spirit of prophecy, begins to flow in your life? Do you know what to do about it, and how to work with others to defeat this enemy spirit?

2. When the Spirit of truth comes into your spirit and your church, what can you expect as far as an enemy

attack? What are the weapons available to you? How do you work with others to deal with it?

3. How does the Spirit of holiness work in the body of Christ, and how does the enemy respond when people are set apart for ministry to train and equip the saints? Do you know how to recognize it and deal with it?

4. What are the signs when the Spirit of life is moving in power? What do you need to do to allow it to flow in you? What should you be preparing to deal with in terms of an enemy attack?

5. How do you recognize the flow of the Spirit of son-ship/adoption? What are the signs that it is moving to the degree that the enemy will respond? What will the enemy's response look like? How do you deal with it?

Hopefully, you have found yourself better prepared for spiritual warfare. Because, like it or not, we are at war and we face a determined and deadly enemy who is trying to expand his territory every day. When we are tested, how will we stand?

As we begin to look at the next of the seven spirits of God, our introduction to this Spirit is very different. It comes as a negative. We are asked to consider the impact of having insulted the Spirit of grace.

*"How much more severely do you think a man deserves to be punished who has trampled the Son of God under foot, who has treated as an unholy thing the blood of the covenant that sanctified him, and who has insulted the Spirit of grace?"* (Hebrews 10:29, NIV)

This scripture delivers a very powerful judgment on people who are actually in the body of Christ. None of these things apply to those outside the body. As I read this again, I am reminded of how much I want to avoid doing any of these things to the Lord. The writer prefaced this quote from Hebrews with this warning:

*"For if we sin willfully after we have received the knowledge of the truth, there no longer remains a sacrifice for sins, but a certain fearful expectation of judgment, and fiery indignation which will devour the adversaries. Anyone who has rejected Moses' law dies without mercy on the testimony of two or three witnesses."* (Hebrews 10:26-28, NIV)

Some think that the Spirit of grace covers everything even if you are disobedient. Perhaps they will have second thoughts after reading this.

In basic training, many things have been spoon fed to the trainees up to this point. When they have been unable to pass tests, they have been told, "Well try it again." The drill sergeants will give them a little hint suggesting a better way to do a task in order to pass the test. But, in the sixth week there is no one giving you hints or letting you do it over again. In the sixth week it is "DO IT OR FAIL!" This is what Paul was saying to the Galatian church. Remember that Paul was talking to the body of the Church when he said, *"You who are trying to be justified by law have been alienated from Christ; you have fallen away from grace."* (Galatians 5:4, NIV) These individuals had gone back to false teaching after accepting the grace of Jesus Christ. These had become alienated and by definition you can't be alienated unless you were once connected. I don't want to fall away from grace or become alienated from Christ! How about you? We must recognize that disobedience tramples Jesus underfoot.

185

Disobedience insults the Spirit of grace. Jesus repeatedly said, "If you are obedient, then I will come and dwell in you and you in me. If you obey me, then the Father will come and we will be united together with Him." If you are obedient, the Spirit of grace comes to you, but if you are disobedient you grieve the Holy Spirit. What happens when you grieve the Holy Spirit? If we grieve the Holy Spirit long enough we may lose that connection. Look at what Paul said to Titus about grace:

*"For the grace of God that brings salvation has appeared to all men. It teaches us to say "No" to ungodliness and worldly passions, and to live self–controlled, upright and godly lives in this present age,"* (Titus 2:11-12)

If you have the Spirit of God as the Spirit of grace, you are going to be learning how to say "No" to all ungodliness. This Spirit will teach you how to be disciplined and obedient. It is important to know that a disobedient, disrespectful soldier will never pass the test. By the end of the sixth week, a disobedient and disrespectful soldier will probably be locked up somewhere and will not even be available to take the test. In our walk with God, we must learn how to respect the Holy Spirit. We must be walking in a way that pleases the Holy Spirit rather than grieving Him. We must learn how to operate with the Spirit of grace.

When we get to this point in our training, we see that there is something very special and unique about this Spirit. Grace is not merely the work of this Spirit, it is the whole battle plan.

## GRACE IS THE OBJECTIVE OF THE ENTIRE BATTLE PLAN

Grace is God's objective for us. At the same time that the Spirit of grace comes to help us accomplish our mission, it is also the objective we have struggled to establish and maintain.

*"And I will pour out on the house of David and the inhabitants of Jerusalem the **spirit of grace** and supplication."* (Zechariah 12:10)

We see here an Old Testament reference to the Spirit of grace. A good definition of grace is "the unmerited favor of God." We don't deserve it. We can't earn it. It is completely unmerited and there is only one source for it. It comes from God.

*"For by grace you have been saved through faith, and that not of yourselves; it is the gift of God, not of works, lest anyone should boast."* (Ephesians 2:8-9)

God's purpose in our ministry is to bring as many of his children home as possible. I like those "God Signs" which appeared on billboards around the country. One of them said, "Why don't you come to my house on Sunday, and bring the kids." God wants us to come home, and our mission is to invite as many as we can to come with us. So, our mission is to bring people to this saving grace; to invite people to come home to their loving Father God.

So much of the church has gone out proclaiming, "Repent or go to hell! If you don't repent, you are going to burn!" But, that's not the way Jesus did it. That's not the way the New Testament evangelists did it. They went out in love filled with grace, and when people experienced that grace through them, they were drawn to Jesus and through Him to Father God. People want love and grace. They are hungry for affection and acceptance. This is a powerful message that needs to be shared with everyone. When people experience that love and grace moving in us they want to know where they can go to get it. Then we have the opportunity to say, "Come and see!"

Our mission is to bring people back to our loving Father, and we must remember that our salvation is a pure work of grace. Our calling is to establish the kingdom of God so that His will is done on earth as it is in heaven. And, that means our most important task is to bring people into the kingdom. But, without the Spirit of grace, all our work is in vain. All of our work is useless without grace.

So we see clearly that grace is BOTH the mission and the means to accomplish the mission. It is by grace alone that we are accounted righteous. Pure, unmerited favor accomplishes what all of our works cannot produce. In Revelation 20:13ff, it says that people will go before the "White Throne" and be "judged, each one according to his works." When I look at that section of scripture, I am reminded that I don't want to be judged according to my works. I want to be judged according to what Jesus did. I want to have His righteousness accredited to my account. I want to come before the throne covered by His blood.

Are you aware that there is an unending supply of grace for those who obey Christ? You can never run out of grace when you are in Christ. If you use some of it, it is immediately replaced and the source is still full. Wouldn't you like to have a gas tank like that? As you drive, the tank keeps filling itself up, and you would never have to look for another gas station or pay the ever increasing prices for fuel. That's how God's grace works. The supply of grace perpetually refills itself for those who are in Christ.

Those in spiritual warfare often quote James 4:7 as their promise for overcoming the devil. However, it is important to keep it the context of the entire passage in order to grasp the full meaning. James 4:7 begins with the word "therefore." As one of my seminary professors would say, "When you encounter a verse beginning with 'therefore' you need to go back and see what it is there for." Carefully note the meaning of this verse in the context of what came before it and what comes after it.

*"But He gives more grace. Therefore He says: "God resists the proud, but gives grace to the humble." Therefore submit to God. Resist the devil and he will flee from you. Draw near to God and He will draw near to you. Cleanse your hands, you sinners; and purify your hearts, you double-minded. Lament and mourn and weep! Let your laughter be turned to mourning and your joy to gloom. Humble yourselves in the sight of the Lord, and He will lift you up."* (James 4:6-10)

First, note that it says God gives more grace. If you need a little more grace today, God will give it. He always has more grace available for us. Next, note that God resists the proud and gives grace to the humble. It is because He gives grace to the humble that we submit to Him. When you submit to God, you are not submitting to some cruel, unfeeling dictatorial authority. You are submitting to the source of more grace. When you fully grasp this, you are enabled with that grace to resist the devil and see him flee from you. Once you are empowered by the grace of God, how hard do you have to fight the devil? You only have to resist and he will flee from you, because you are grace filled, and empowered by the Spirit of grace.

It is equally important to study what comes after verse 7. We must learn to draw near to God. Remember as a child how safe you felt when you were near your parents. Multiply that by an infinite number and you begin to sense how safe you are when near Father God. However, to get there and stay there, you need to cleanse your hands and purify your heart. Double minded people don't receive more grace. They disqualify themselves. You can't believe for it and doubt it at the same time. You can't submit to God and stay submitted to principalities and powers. You must make up your mind, humble yourself in the eyes of God and let him lift you up.

In combat, resupply is one of the most critical elements of the process. Military history is filled with accounts of armies moving too far from their source of resupply. You can only carry so much weight. This limits the amount of ammunition you are able to take with you. When your supply runs low, you need to be able to receive a resupply quickly in order to remain successful. With the advanced equipment available today, an army can move forward at a high rate of speed, but must never go beyond the resupply lines. Many battles in the past were lost because resupply efforts failed.

The Spirit of grace is your supply line in spiritual warfare. You can be certain that the Spirit of grace will never fail to provide what you need. Through this Spirit, God will never let you run out of supplies. Thanks be to God! So, don't ever let anything take the Spirit of grace from you. When you do, you have cut yourself off from the flow.

> *"As God's fellow workers we urge you not to receive God's grace in vain. For he says, "In the time of my favor I heard you, and in the day of salvation I helped you." I tell you, now is the time of God's favor, now is the day of salvation."* (2 Corinthians 6:1-2, NIV)

Think about the first four words in this passage. We are God's fellow workers. We are God's team members. We are working with Him and He is working with us. We are on the same fire team. Think about the power that comes to you when God is on your team. But the passage warns us of a terrible reality. We can receive God's grace in vain. If we don't value it and honor it, we can lose it. Remember Paul's warning to the Galatians,

> *"You have become estranged from Christ, you who attempt to be justified by law; you have fallen from grace."* (Galatians 5:4)

It is such good news that God sends the Spirit of grace to battle for us and with us. What an awesome addition to our friendly forces. But, you know that every good news story also has a "bad news" element. It is the same in the area of spiritual warfare. The bad news is that the enemy tries to disrupt the flow and hinder our progress. He always responds to a move of God.

## WHEN THE SPIRIT OF GRACE COMES
## THE ENEMY RESPONDS

As you study the Old Testament, you read about different idols which people have worshipped through the centuries. Many people believe that such things are in the past and for-gotten. They erroneously believe that no one is affected by those idols today. But, that is not true. The false gods men-tioned in the Bible didn't just go away. Every one of them had a demon behind it. These are prince demons and they do not die. Even in the lake of fire, they are not going to die. We are told in the book of revelation that they will burn forever. They are going to be given a body that can burn forever without being consumed. These principalities do not just go away, and these prince demons do not die.

When you read about those idols, no matter which type they may have been, they had wicked spirits behind them that are still alive and still working. Some idols were made of stone. Others carved from wood. Still others were molded of gold or silver. They had different names and claimed different powers. But, they all had one thing in common. There was a demon spirit behind them using its power to lure people away from God. We must be aware of this fact. Study the scripture to verify this. I am providing a couple of passages for you here.

*"What am I saying then? That an idol is anything, or what is offered to idols is anything? Rather, that the*

*things which the Gentiles sacrifice they sacrifice to __demons__ and not to God, and I do not want you to have fellowship with __demons__. You cannot drink the cup of the Lord and the cup of __demons__; you cannot partake of the Lord's table and of the table of __demons__."* (1 Corinthians 10:19-21)

*"They even sacrificed their sons and their daughters to __demons__, And shed innocent blood, the blood of their sons and daughters, whom they sacrificed to the idols of Canaan; and the land was polluted with blood."* (Psalm 106:37-38

Always remember that each one of these idols had a wicked prince demon behind it which is still alive and working today. The spirit (principality) that comes to block the Spirit of grace is Baal or more correctly the demonic principality behind Baal.

The spirit behind Baal is the Prince of Persia. This is a very powerful, vicious, and wicked spirit. This spirit was in control of all the powers opposed to God in that whole region. It is the spirit that hindered the answer to Daniel's prayers for twenty one days. Reading the scriptures, you learn that Michael, the archangel protecting Israel, came to the aid of Gabriel when he was fighting against the Prince of Persia. Michael is a powerful archangel who will one day take Satan captive. He came to help Gabriel wrestle that demonic spirit known as the Prince of Persia. It is important to realize that when you go up against the Prince of Persia, you are not dealing with some tired old minor demon. You are dealing with one of the most powerful of all the principalities.

When I first prepared to teach this section, I was not fully prepared for the way this spirit comes against us. I had more spiritual warfare at that time than at any other time in my walk with Christ. It came against me from so many directions at the same time. At first, I was taken off guard. It was painful at the time, but God turned it into something good. I learned a very important lesson about dealing with these spirits. They don't want to be talked about. They don't want you to study about them and learn what to do when you are under attack. They want to use their power behind the scenes so that they can literally get away with murder.

I experienced the same kind of attacks when I began to write this chapter. For the better part of three days things came against me which seemed unrelated to this work. However, as I went back to the Lord for strength and understanding, I saw clearly what had happened. So prepare yourself for increased warfare with each successive lesson. But, don't be tempted to give up. These spirits will come against you whether you study about them or not. The difference is that when you understand what is happening, you know how to deal with it. Remaining ignorant of the work of demons will not protect you from their destructive warfare. The enemy has declared war and he plans to steal, kill and destroy. Lift the veil and fight like a disciple of Jesus Christ!

This demonic spirit is so strong that even a powerful man like Daniel was hindered. Daniel had such a close connection with God that his prayers went straight to the Lord and were immediately answered. However, this prince demon was able to delay the answers in the life of this righteous man.

As you study the principality behind Baal, it is important to note that Baal was the god Jezebel worshipped. When they study Jezebel, most people get nervous and concerned about what this spirit can do. Now, we are looking at a spirit (a principality) which was so much more powerful than Jezebel that she worshipped it. When she looked at Baal, she said, "Now, that is a god!" If you think it was tough dealing with Jezebel, consider the challenge of dealing with Baal. One of the reasons Jezebel is so successful is that Baal is the prince demon over the spirit of Jezebel, and as such, it is much more wicked than Jezebel.

Because these spirits are very strong, many avoid talking about them. There is a false belief that if you don't mention them they will go away. So, why am I teaching people about these spirits? If they don't want to be exposed, why not just be quiet about them? One reason I am compelled to teach this, is that God told me to do it, and you need to know the truth. The second reason is that whether you know it or not, these spirits will come against you when you begin to move in the power of God released by the seven Spirits. Instead of running away and hiding in fear, you need to wake up every day stomping on demons. Every morning when you wake up, Hell ought to tremble in fear. Demons should scurry for cover like the legion Jesus met in the country of the Gadarenes. We need to become aware of the authority we have in Christ over the enemy.

*"And He said to them, "I saw Satan fall like lightning from heaven. Behold, I give you the authority to trample on serpents and scorpions, and over all the power of the enemy, and nothing shall by any means hurt you."* (Luke 10:18-19)

How much of the power of the enemy has Jesus given us authority over? He has given us authority over "ALL" the power of the enemy. It is time for you to stop letting these little demons have authority over you and by your own confession empowering them to oppression you. It is time to stop letting these big demons have so much power and authority over you. It is time for you to rise up in the authority Jesus gave and take them out. It is time to wrestle with principalities and cast out demons in the power and authority of Jesus Christ. Amen?

But, many of us are kept down and held in check by Baal. He has so effectively kept the church down that most of the members don't even know who he is. They don't understand how he works or what to do with him. In the midst of all this confusion and deception, he has held us in check for far too long.

As you study about Baal, you will find that he has always been connected with wealth, prosperity, financial security, and the economy. In the Old Testament, we see that people believed Baal would bless their fields, their flocks, and their families. They came to believe that he was the source of all blessing. So, Baal was always connected with fruitfulness, prosperity, and reproduction. In the minds of primitive people, all of these were dependent on Baal.

Baal worship involved sexual immorality, fertility rites, and the sins of the flesh. Considering this, look at where we are today. Even in our churches among the members and the leaders, people are being caught up in these spirits and are brought down by them. This is all part of the enemy's plan to destroy your work. Baal worship was so bad that God literally cast those who worshipped him out of the land. People who got caught up in this were no longer worthy to live in the good land. The Bible says that God spewed them out - almost like regurgitating. People would become so wicked that the only solution was to eliminate them. If they moved to another location, they would lead the people there into the same abominations. It was like a contagious disease which had to be isolated and destroyed.

One of the reasons God hated Baal worship so much was that it had to do with child sacrifice. All children belong to God, and when they are sacrificed, it is God's children who are murdered. Even the kings of Israel and Judah got involved in this and sacrificed their children in the fire. They gave their own heirs to demon spirits. Can you imagine the grief God felt when He saw His children being burned alive in their unholy fire. Most of us would like to proudly say, "Well at least we don't do that sort of thing today!" But, think about it. What is behind the widespread practice of abortion today? Why is it so difficult to stop this practice and break the power of worldly support for it? It is Baal who leads people to sacrifice the next generation for their own prosperity, health, and comfort. Baal encourages you to have all the pleasures of the flesh and then simply sacrifice the consequences for your own welfare. I firmly believe that abortion is a sacrifice to Baal. Think about the reasons given for abortion. "We can't afford to have a baby right now." We see in this that wealth is tied to child sacrifice. (Baal has to do with prosperity)."

Baal worship is so wicked because it leads people to connect with Baal and break their connection with God. It is a rejection of the Lord of glory and all that He has planned for you. It is a powerful statement of lacking faith that God can and will take care of you.

The name Baal has several meanings. One of the meanings is ownership. Baal wants to own everything. He promises to provide for you, but he doesn't come through, because he wants it all. When you receive from him, you will quickly find that he takes it all back and leaves you with nothing. The name Baal also means ruler. He wants to rule everything. He even rules over Jezebel. Another meaning for the name Baal is master. When you give in to him, you will find that he is the master and you are the slave. The name also means possessor, and he intends to possess everything.

The Hebrew word which was translated as Baal, actually means husband. Interestingly the name Jezebel means "without husband." In the first lesson, we looked at her relationship with Ahab. In reality, she was married to Baal rather than Ahab.

You can see this more clearly when you realize that the worship of Baal always involved marriage ceremonies. To be accepted as a true follower of Baal, you had to go through these ceremonies and confess that you were married to Baal. Then, it was believed, you could partake of what was his. You married into provision, prosperity, power, and privilege.

Now you can see what the spirit of Baal really wants. He wants the bride of Christ to be his bride. He plans to win her by stealing her affection. He wants her to believe that she can't really count on the Lord to meet her needs and protect her from harm. He uses those troubling little questions about her past attempting to get her to believe that God was not really with her during the difficult times. He wants to get the bride to begin questioning whether Jesus can and will take care of her during times of tribulation and suffering. Perhaps you have experienced times when these questions just kept coming up. You didn't want to ask them. You didn't want to mistrust Christ, but you kept hearing those questions in your spirit. That was the spirit of Baal working against you.

The symbol of Baal is a bull. Now, think about this in our world today. Even today, we call a strong market a "bull" market. One investment firm has a bull as the symbol of their ability to provide wealth and increase for you. We have become so compromised and deceived that we use these things in our every day conversations without knowing what we are really saying. We begin to believe that if we get connected to this world's economic system, a bull market is going to provide wealth and security for our future. It is the spirit of Baal behind it all, and his victims are not even aware of his presence or what he plans for them. Once in a while, we actually need an economic crash to help people realize that Baal is a liar and cannot be trusted. Baal can't really provide prosperity.

Baal is so bold and so brash that he pushes his claims even further. He says that he is the source of your blessings. He will try to convince you that when you don't feel blessed, God is withholding from you. Baal wants you to believe that if you commit to him, he will meet all your needs. If you don't commit to him, he will try to hold up your blessings from God as he held up the answers to Daniel's prayers.

When you reject him and stay connected with the Lord, Baal tries to block your income and hinder the financial flow in your business, investments, and savings. He tries to block sales. He will come against you when you are trying to make a sale. If he finds a weakness in your customers, he will try to exploit that to block your prosperity. He will work to stop or delay the monetary transfers you need for your personal accounts and your business accounts.

Baal will try to block the flow of your God given prosperity in life. Baal tries to convince people that God is a liar and that God does not provide for their needs. He wants you to mistrust Jehovah Jireh, the God who provides, and to believe that the only one you can trust is Baal.

When the Israelites moved into the land formerly held by worshippers of Baal, they said that it was God who provided the rain and increase. Think about how this assertion struck the Baal followers. It was a huge insult to their belief system and it led to war. Each side claimed that it was their God who sent the rain, blessed the crops, and produced prosperity. Even today, Baal doesn't want you to believe that God supplies all your needs.

When the Israelites were given the "promised land," they were supposed to destroy Baal worship, but instead, they started intermarrying into the Baal family. The temptations are great. It is a virtue in Baal worship to participate in all the pleasures of the flesh. One by one, they started to participate in the fertility rites and became totally caught up in it. Judges were brought up by the Lord to destroy the practices, but the next generation would fall again. Eventually, the Lord removed the Israelites from the land. After 70 years of captivity, many finally returned to the land, and some of them were lured right back into the terrible religious system of Baal. We see that the people of Israel were still tied to Baal in the time of Ezra, Nehemiah, and in the New Testament Church. In the Revelation of John, we find it at work in the seven churches which represent the church again. It is back in the form of the doctrine of the Nicolaitans, and Jesus proclaims that He hates this practice. The shocking fact is that servitude to Baal is a reality in the church and the world today.

Some things are difficult to understand in the Bible without this background in the demon spirits which work in these idolatrous practices. Imagine the effect on Baal worshippers when Elijah prayed, and there was no rain for three and a half years. Their great claim was that Baal was the source of rain, but this prophet of God came with a declaration that Baal had no control over the rain and that the God of heaven was the only one who could make it rain. Elijah offered a demonstration. He asked God in prayer to stop the rain and God shut the heavens over Israel for three and a half years. That's a very long object lesson, and the message was very clear. After Elijah defeated the prophets of Baal on Mount Carmel, he prayed again, and the rains returned. This was a powerful attack on the worship of Baal by one man who was empowered by the Spirit of God. One person today can bring down Baal with the power of the Spirit of grace.

If you fall for his deception and begin to let Baal operate in your life, one of the things he will do is make you feel inferior. He wants to intimidate you to the point that you will no longer resist. We get a lesson on his tactics and their debilitating effect in the story of Gideon.

*"Then the children of Israel did evil in the sight of the Lord. So the Lord delivered them into the hand of Midian for seven years, and the hand of Midian prevailed against Israel. Because of the Midianites, the children of Israel made for themselves the dens, the caves, and the strongholds which are in the mountains. So it was, whenever Israel had sown, Midianites would come up; also Amalekites and the people of the East would come up against them. Then they would encamp against them and destroy the produce of the earth as far as Gaza, and leave no sustenance for Israel, neither sheep nor ox nor donkey. For they would come up with their livestock and their tents, coming in as numerous as locusts;*

*both they and their camels were without number; and
they would enter the land to destroy it. So Israel was
greatly impoverished because of the Midianites, and the
children of Israel cried out to the Lord. And it came to
pass, when the children of Israel cried out to the Lord
because of the Midianites, that the Lord sent a prophet
to the children of Israel, who said to them, "Thus says
the Lord God of Israel: 'I brought you up from Egypt
and brought you out of the house of bondage; and I
delivered you out of the hand of the Egyptians and out
of the hand of all who oppressed you, and drove them
out before you and gave you their land. Also I said to
you, "I am the Lord your God; do not fear the gods of
the Amorites, in whose land you dwell." But you have
not obeyed My voice.'"* (Judges 6:1-10)

The god of the Amorites was Baal. The spirit behind Baal
wants to keep you in bondage to fear and keep you in hiding so
you will not resist him. He had lured the Israelites away from
trusting and serving God, and then he enslaved them. In the
time of Gideon, Israel had been reduced to hiding in clefts in
the rocks, caves and strongholds. Their enemies would come
in at harvest time and steal or destroy their crops (see John
10:10). They felt powerless to deal with all these enemies, and
simply tried to exist at the survival level. The days of prosperity were gone, because Baal had lied to them, and like every
manifestation of the enemy he was working to steal, kill and
destroy them.

The same sorts of things happen in the world today. In
some of our marriages, in the jobs we have, and the churches
we attend, people are constantly kept down, intimidated, and
pushed into hiding. When this happens in a church, a work-
place, or in a family, it is the spirit of Baal which is behind it.
Knowing all of this, how do we deal with a spirit of Baal when
it comes against us?

# HOW TO DEAL WITH THE SPIRIT OF BAAL?

First of all, we've got to stop believing that church is like a hobby or social club where we can just play at its business and activities. We've got to start telling the truth about spiritual warfare and the demonic spirits (the principalities) which are coming to oppose us. We have to give up this whole notion that we can please God with large crowds in seeker sensitive churches which don't tell it like it is. By remaining overly sensitive and valuing inclusion above truth, these churches fail to properly train their people for warfare.

The gospel of Jesus Christ has always offended people. Jesus was an offense to the Pharisees, Sadducees, political leaders, and self-righteous people everywhere. In reality it is much more insensitive to send sheep into packs of wolves believing there is no danger because we are too modern to believe these old stories. Satan is real! Principalities and powers are real! Demons are real! Jesus wasn't lying to us when He talked about them. The Bible is not antiquated because it discuses them. It is a violation of our duty in all of the five offices of ministry if we don't warn and prepare our people.

We need to take off the rose colored glasses and face the truth. I remember getting a prescription for new glasses and when I picked them up the lens were actually rose colored. I tell you the truth. I didn't want to wear rose colored glasses then, and I certainly don't want to wear them now. But, the enemy wants you to put on those rose colored glasses and only see what he wants you to see. He wants you to be blind to some of the real dangers in this world. Listen to Jude's warning to the church!

*"For certain men have crept in unnoticed, who long ago were marked out for this condemnation, ungodly men, who turn the grace of our God into lewdness and deny*

*the only Lord God and our Lord Jesus Christ.*" (Jude 1:4)

Jude is describing Baal. This is what Baal does. We must remember that we have a real enemy, and we are at war. We must start telling the truth about it. And we begin by examining ourselves and ridding our lives of all attachments to Baal. If you have fallen for any of these deceptions, call on the Lord to send the Spirit of grace and break the power of Baal off of you. If you are trusting more in money for your future security than you are trusting in God, you need the Spirit of grace. If you have fallen for the deception that it is okay to participate in the pleasures of the flesh and trust the world to provide what you need, that is Baal. You need for God to break his strangle hold on you through the work of the Spirit of grace. This is critical. It is literally a matter of life and death.

As we have studied in previous lessons, being able to identify the enemy is a critical combat skill. In basic training, they teach target recognition. Soldiers need to be able to look at a silhouette of a tank or a jet and know if it belongs to the enemy or to our friendly forces. There are powerful weapons of warfare available today. There is a shoulder held anti-tank weapon that can totally devastate the most powerful and heavily armored tanks on the battlefield. When you hit a tank with one of these weapons it is completely destroyed. If you go to the tank to check on it, you will find pieces scattered over a 1500 meter area. Because of this devastating effect, you don't want to hit one of your own tanks or one belonging to an ally. It tends to upset our allies when we destroy their vehicles. You have to be able to recognize the enemy and all of his weapons. This is what we are talking about here. Can you recognize the enemy and follow his movements? Do you know who he is and how he has disguised himself today?

One thing that can help you to recognize Baal is to get a handle on the meaning of his various names. These names give you a clue that you can use for target recognition. One of Baal's names is Baal-hamon which means "the lord of wealth or abundance." It is a counterfeit of Jehovah Jireh. If you are highly focused on attaining wealth in this world, you are vulnerable to this aspect of Baal. There is nothing wrong with money or wealth if it is properly received and righteously used. It is the love of money which is the root of evil. Baal wants you to love and lust after wealth. This spirit like all enemy spirits is a liar. To be effective in spiritual warfare, you must know who the real source of abundance is, how to recognize him, and how to get into the flow of blessings coming from Him. Your only real source of abundance is God. Remember what Jesus said about the enemy, and what he said about himself.

*"The thief does not come except to steal, and to kill, and to destroy. I have come that they may have life, and that they may have it more abundantly."* (John 10:10)

Baal-berith is another of his names, and means "the lord of the covenant." This is a counterfeit spirit. He has no power over the covenant. Our God is the God of the covenant, and not Baal.

As mentioned earlier, the Hebrew word baal sometimes actually means "husband" or "marriage." This is a counterfeit marriage. It is not legal and cannot produce the desired results. Our Bridegroom is Jesus Christ our savior. Now compare these names for Baal with the names for our God:

| | |
|---|---|
| ELOHIM...Genesis 1:1, Psalm 19:1, 8:5 | "God of power and might" |
| ADONAI......Malachi 1:6 | "Lord" |
| JEHOVAH—YAHWEH..... Genesis 2:4 | "God of our salvation." |

| | |
|---|---|
| JEHOVAH-ROHI....Psalm 23:1 | "The Lord my shepherd" |
| JEHOVAH-SHAMMAH...Ezek 48:35 | "The Lord who is present" |
| JEHOVAH-RAPHA...Exodus 15:26 | "The Lord our healer" |
| JEHOVAH-JIREH...Genesis 22:13-14 | "The Lord will provide" |
| JEHOVAH-NISSI...Exodus 17:15 | "The Lord our banner" |
| JEHOVAH-SHALOM.....Judges 6:24 | "The Lord our peace" |
| JEHOVAH-SABBAOTH...Isaiah 6:1-3 | "The Lord of Hosts" |
| JEHOVAH-TSIDKENU... Jeremiah 23:6 | "The Lord our Righteousness" |
| EL-SHADDAI...Genesis 17:1, Psalm 91:1 | "God Almighty" |
| YAHWEH...Genesis 4:3; Exodus 6:3; 3:12 | "The God who is" |

God gave us all these names so that we could know His character and recognize His work. He gave us these names to teach us to trust in Him and turn to Him as the source of our supply and the one who meets all our needs.

The best way to deal with Baal is to get divorced from him and all attachments to him (see the divorce at Appendix B). If you want to be the bride of Christ, you must stop being the bride of Baal. You must be in the process of preparing yourself as the bride of Christ by getting adorned with His holiness, His righteousness, and the jewels the Holy Spirit brings to you.

You must know and affirm that God is your source, and He will give you the strength to overcome. God will be with you! God will provide for all your need! Remember what happened to Israel. As soon as they became attached to Baal, they were hiding in the clefts of the rocks and in caves. They were without food because the stronger forces serving Baal were now stealing their supply.

You must realize that in spiritual warfare it is all or none. When you go to war there is no tie or draw. You either win or lose. You either live or you die. There is no middle ground. You either belong to God living in the freedom of His Spirit or you belong to Baal in bondage to fear and deprivation. That is why Joshua's challenge to Israel when they faced the Amorites was so significant to them and remains significant to us.

*"Now therefore, fear the Lord, serve Him in sincerity and in truth, and put away the gods which your fathers served on the other side of the River and in Egypt. Serve the Lord! And if it seems evil to you to serve the Lord, choose for yourselves this day whom you will serve, whether the gods which your fathers served that were on the other side of the River, or the gods of the Amorites, in whose land you dwell. But as for me and my house, we will serve the Lord."* (Joshua 24:14-15)

Baal was the God of the Amorites. This is a choice that we each must make. As for me and my household, we will serve the Lord. Amen?

## TO PLEASE GOD WE MUST SERVE HIM AND HIM ALONE.

The Lord God made it clear that He is a jealous God. He commanded us to have no other gods before Him. We should learn this lesson and never try to have any other gods standing beside Him. Israel tried that and it didn't work. And, I can guarantee you that it will not work for you today. In these last days, we need to be bold in the Spirit of grace. Remember in Acts 4 when the disciples prayed for boldness. God let loose a second outpouring of the Holy Spirit. It was so powerful the house shook. If you pray for boldness through the power and presence of the Holy Spirit, God will provide. Have you noticed the end result of this prayer.

*"And with great power the apostles gave witness to the resurrection of the Lord Jesus. And great grace was upon them all."* (Acts 4:33)

In these last days it is essential that we know the Word of God. We must know our Bibles, and have them stored in our hearts. When the enemy comes you may not have a Bible with you. The only weapon you have against his attack is the Word stored in your heart. Remember that the Word is the Sword of the Spirit.

More than at any time in the past, we need to be led by the Holy Spirit. We need to be familiar with the seven Spirits of God and know how to call upon them and fight along with them in the battles ahead. We need to know how they lead us, what they do for us, how we cooperate with them, and how we employ them in times of war. We must know who we are in Christ, and we need to know whose we are.

God has provided many great lessons in our soldier's manual (BIBLE). We must learn these lessons and apply the principles in our lives. There is a great lesson in the book of Judges when the Angel of the Lord visited Gideon. The people had not been willing to listen to the prophet sent by God. So, God sent an angel. Have you noticed that when God sends an angel (especially the Angel of the Lord) things change. Great power is released with the visit of this Angel. If God sends you an angel, you really need to listen.

*"Now the Angel of the Lord came and sat under the terebinth tree which was in Ophrah, which belonged to Joash the Abiezrite, while his son Gideon threshed wheat in the winepress, in order to hide it from the Midianites. And the Angel of the Lord appeared to him, and said to him, "The Lord is with you, you mighty man of valor!" Gideon said to Him, "O my lord, if the Lord is with us, why then has all this happened to us? And where are all His miracles which our fathers told us about, saying, 'Did not the Lord bring us up from Egypt?' But now the Lord has forsaken us and delivered us into the hands of the Midianites." Then the Lord turned to him and said, "Go in this might of yours, and you shall save Israel from the hand of the Midianites. Have I not sent you?" So he said to Him, "O my Lord, how can I save Israel? Indeed my clan is the weakest in Manasseh, and I am the least in my father's house." And the Lord said to him, "Surely I will be with you, and you shall defeat the Midianites as one man." (Judges 6:11-16)*

Baal had pushed Gideon down. Gideon thought he was the least of the least. God had a different image of Gideon. He saw Gideon as a mighty warrior. He sees you as a mighty warrior even if you can't see it for yourself. Do you know that together you and the Lord are a powerful team? The problem in Gideon's story was not God's failure, but Israel's ties to Baal. A bold new Gideon tore down Baal's altars and burned them.

*"Then the men of the city said to Joash, "Bring out your son, that he may die, because he has torn down the altar of Baal, and because he has cut down the wooden image that was beside it." But Joash said to all who stood against him, "Would you plead for Baal? Would you save him? Let the one who would plead for him be put to*

*death by morning! If he is a god, let him plead for him-self, because his altar has been torn down!" Therefore on that day he called him Jerubbaal, saying, "Let Baal plead against him, because he has torn down his altar." Then all the Midianites and Amalekites, the people of the East, gathered together; and they crossed over and encamped in the Valley of Jezreel. But the Spirit of the Lord came upon Gideon; then he blew the trumpet, and the Abiezrites gathered behind him."* (Judges 6:30-34)

**KEY CONCEPT**: Don't expect much support from those who are sold out to Baal. They want to hold on to the pleasures of Baal, and they will try to kill you if you interfere with their idols. You need to remember who is on your side and who you can count on when you are at war.

It's time for the church of Jesus Christ to rise up and take a stand. It's time to say, "NO!" to Baal in every aspect of this abomination. If you want to be the bride of Christ, cast off Baal forever. Understand who you are: a person of authority under God.

This is war, and you are either with Jesus or against Him. You either stand for what is righteous and holy or you stand for Baal and his corrupt worldly system. We must begin to call things what they really are. We must call sexual immorality what it is. It is submission to Baal. We must call perversions what they are. They are submission to Baal. We must call abortion what it is. It is submission to Baal and represents a sacrifice of our children to the detestable god Molech.

You must choose this day and every day "whom you will serve." This is not some long forgotten Old Testament problem that disappeared years ago. The prince of Persia is alive today. He is operating in our world, and he wants you to fall in love with him. The veil of deception is very strong. And you must know that it will get stronger as the return of Jesus gets closer.

We must be aware that we too can fall to this spirit. Remember these words of Jesus:

*"For false Christs and false prophets will appear and perform great signs and miracles to deceive even the elect—if that were possible. See, I have told you ahead of time."* (Matthew 24:24-25, NIV)

We must stand fast with the Spirit of Grace! We must allow the Spirit of grace to flow. We must let the Lord's salvation come. We must let the Spirit of Grace remove all the stains of sin, all the shame from our past. If you are holding on to any shame from your past, Baal will use it against you to keep you in hiding where you cannot block his work. You need to realize that it was nailed to the cross of Jesus Christ and it is gone forever. God has chosen to cover it and not to remember it any more. Now, you need to let it go so it can't be used against you by these wicked spirits.

You need to stand and make some decrees which will establish you in your relationship with Jesus. Speak these decrees out loud with authority.

All my sins and shame were nailed to the cross of Jesus Christ and they are gone forever!

I am now the bride of Jesus Christ, a new creation, and I am no longer the person who did any of those things!

I have been born again! I am a new creation, and those old things have nothing to do with me.

Jesus took it all, and the veil of deception is gone! I am standing with Jesus! I am going to recognize my groom! I am going to follow my groom!

I am married to Jesus Christ, and I reject Baal and all attachments to him!

## PRAYER TO BREAK ALL TIES WITH BAAL

Father God, I thank you that you send the Spirit of Grace to reconcile us to our real groom. You sent the Spirit of truth to break through our confusion and help us to see what is real, and to know when we are being tempted and tested to pull away from you and move toward Baal. I ask you to release a powerful impartation of the Spirit of truth and the Spirit of grace. Lord, help us today to be completely divorced from Baal and all our attachments to him. We are not looking to him for anything. He is not the source of our supply, he is not the source of rain, he is not the source of water, he is not the source of fertility, and he is not the source of anything for us. You, Father God, are our source, and we turn to you, open and ready to receive the flow of living water through your Spirit of grace. We want to be faithful to Jesus and to be channels through which rivers of living water can flow into a dry and thirsty land. To accomplish these things, we need even more of your Spirit of grace, and we ask you to release it to us now and keep it flowing through us forever. We ask it in the mighty name of Yeshua ha Messiach. Amen and Amen!

## ADDITIONAL SCRIPTURES FOR PERSONAL STUDY

Psalm 5:12 (NIV), "For surely, O LORD, you bless the righteous; you surround them with your favor as with a shield."

Psalm 30:5 (NIV), "For his anger lasts only a moment, but his favor lasts a lifetime; weeping may remain for a night, but rejoicing comes in the morning."

Psalm 69:13 (NIV), "But I pray to you, O LORD, in the time of your favor; in your great love, O God, answer me with your sure salvation."

Psalm 84:11 (NKJV), "For the Lord God *is* a sun and shield; The Lord will give grace and glory; No good *thing* will He withhold From those who walk uprightly."

Psalm 90:17 (NIV), "May the favor of the Lord our God rest upon us; establish the work of our hands for us—yes, establish the work of our hands."

## NOTES

# "THE SPIRIT OF GLORY"

During the American Civil War, the commander of the army of the South would ride his magnificent white horse back and forth across the battlefield exposing himself to enemy fire. In times when morale was low and fear was high, General Robert E. Lee would move back and forth through the troop lines and inspire the soldiers to renewed hope and determination. It was as if the glory of the South was being paraded before their eyes and the entire army would begin to give mighty shouts of victory. They would let loose their famous rebel yell and seemingly shift the atmosphere on the battlefield. This would often send fear through the armies of the North, but for some reason no northern soldier ever capitalized on General Lee's vulnerability.

In an even more grand way the Lord of Hosts sends His Holy Spirit to all those caught up in spiritual warfare releasing great assurance to each of them of the final victory. The Holy Spirit parades back and forth across the battlefield inspiring the armies of the Lord to new levels of courage and confidence. There is nothing like the power of the presence of the Lord to build up, strengthen, comfort and empower those who are on the front lines of the greatest struggle in all of human history. And this is where you and I stand today. We are those soldiers who have enlisted in the army of the Lord, and now find ourselves positioned on the front lines of the most significant battle which will ever be fought to determine the destiny of a people set free through the mighty work of our King of kings and Lord of lords, Jesus Christ.

We must never forget that we are at war with a determined and relentless enemy. He wants to steal everything we have, kill our physical bodies, and destroy all our work for the Commander in Chief, Jesus Christ. We only have two choices: fight or die. Remember what Jesus said,

*"The thief comes only in order to steal and kill and destroy. I came that they may have and enjoy life, and have it in abundance (to the full, till it overflows)."* (John 10:10, AMP)

Jesus makes the enemy's intent and our choices very clear. We can choose to let the enemy go on stealing, killing, and destroying, or we can choose to have life "in abundance, to the full, till it overflows." Our choices are clear. The enemy's goals are clear, and he is determined to accomplish these goals by constantly being on the offensive against us. To survive, we must learn how to wage spiritual warfare against these constant attacks. Knowing that we will have constant enemy assaults on us, our families, and our churches, we need to make the decision now to get prepared and stay prepared for the battle in which we now find ourselves.

## IT IS CRITICALLY IMPORTANT TO STAY ALERT

How many times did Jesus tell us that we must stay on watch. Remember Luke 21:36, "Watch therefore, and pray always that you may be counted worthy to escape all these things that will come to pass, and to stand before the Son of Man." We must never let down our guard. We must listen to our Commander in Chief and remain watchful and ready for an enemy attack which could come at any moment.

The apostle Peter knew very clearly what it was like to let down your guard and let the enemy come in during a critical moment. He knew what it was like to be the victim of a sneak attack by the enemy. In his human pride, he was confident that he had risen above being deceived by the enemy. However, none of us will enjoy that privilege until Jesus returns to set up His millennial reign. In the meantime, Peter gives us a strong warning:

*"Be sober, be vigilant; because your adversary the devil walks about like a roaring lion, seeking whom he may devour. Resist him, steadfast in the faith, knowing that the same sufferings are experienced by your brotherhood in the world. But may the God of all grace, who called us to His eternal glory by Christ Jesus, after you have suffered a while, perfect, establish, strengthen, and settle you."* (1 Peter 5:8-10)

It is true that we must remain self-controlled and alert. However, we must also be prepared to deal with the deception of the enemy. We must not fall for his deceitful tricks. He is not really a lion. He is a defeated foe who tries to counterfeit everything of the Lord in order to exploit our weaknesses. Jesus is the lion. Jesus is the Lion of the tribe of Judah, and the devil is just a cheap counterfeit. He is a defeated foe. Remember Jesus' words:

*"And He said to them, "I saw Satan fall like lightning from heaven. Behold, I give you the authority to trample on serpents and scorpions, and over all the power of the enemy, and nothing shall by any means hurt you."* (Luke 10:18-19)

Don't fall for the enemy's deception and don't believe his lies and tricks. We must remember to avoid listening to his words. He wants to give us a spirit of fear and lure us back into bondage to sin and death. Paul soundly warned his spiritual son in 2 Timothy 1:7 (NKJV), "For God has not given us a spirit of fear, but of power and of love and of a sound mind." The devil wants to replace your faith with his fear. He wants to replace your sound mind with his confusion. It is essential in times of war to avoid listening to enemy propaganda. Military forces throughout history have attempted to weaken their enemies by instilling fear in those on the battlefield. We must not fall for this age old trick during our watch. To remain strong and to be of good courage, remember who is on your side. To get the full and correct meaning of one key passage, we need to look at it in more than one translation.

*"From the west, men will fear the name of the LORD, and from the rising of the sun, they will revere his glory. For he will come like a pent-up flood that the breath of the LORD drives along."* (Isaiah 59:19, NIV)

*"So shall they fear the name of the Lord from the west, and His glory from the rising of the sun; when the enemy comes in like a flood, the Spirit of the Lord will lift up a standard against him."* (Isaiah 59:19)

Notice that the NKJV and some other older versions attribute the power of a flood to the enemy. This is a translator's mistake. There were no commas or other punctuation marks in the original languages. The translator placed the comma in the wrong place as evidenced by later translations of the original texts. It should say, "when the enemy comes in, like a flood the Spirit of the Lord will lift up a standard against him." People continually attribute more power and authority to the devil than he deserves. We must learn and remember that he is a defeated foe, and the Lord has given us authority over all his power and alleged ability to harm us. We must learn to continually confess what Jesus said. By confessing His Word, we build up our faith and bring the power of the promises into our situation. Confess again (out loud) several times the authority Jesus has given you.

*"And He said to them, 'I saw Satan fall like lightning from heaven. Behold, I give you the authority to trample on serpents and scorpions, and over all the power of the enemy, and nothing shall by any means hurt you.'"* (Luke 10:18-19)

God has never and will never leave us without any defenses, support, or weapons. We have His published operations order: the Bible. He provides His powerful presence on the battlefield to inspire and encourage us. He sends the Holy Spirit with supernatural power to defend and protect us as well as to equip and support us during every battle we will face. He has sent these "nuclear class" weapons of spiritual warfare to fight alongside our forces.

During one tour of duty, I was the chaplain for a "Weapons Support Detachment" which was tasked to control and fire nuclear weapons. Every six months they went through a "Nuclear Surety Test" to demonstrate their qualifications. If one step in the process of arming and firing one of these weapons was missed, the unit failed and the officer in charge was relieved of duty. If one step in the process was completed at the wrong time, the officer in charge was relieved of duty. Being relieved of duty in one of these units was a career terminating event. It is so critically important to handle nuclear class weapons with great respect, care, and accuracy. There is no room for error. We need to learn the same kind of respect, care, and concern in handling the seven Spirits of God.

These very powerful weapons are the seven Spirits of God sent out into all the world by our 7 Star General, Jesus Christ. Look again at the cornerstone passage for this training found in Revelation 5.

> *"And I looked, and behold, in the midst of the throne and of the four living creatures, and in the midst of the elders, stood a Lamb as though it had been slain, having seven horns and seven eyes, which are the seven Spirits of God sent out into all the earth."* (Revelation 5:6)

So far we have looked at six (6) of these seven (7) Spirits of God. It is important to remember who they are and what they do for us. You need to know how to call on them in your times of need and to know what you should do to support their work and stay out of the way when it is appropriate. You must also be aware of which principalities the enemy sends against these seven Spirits so that you are not surprised or stunned by his actions. Can you name the seven Spirits of God without reading them from the book? I have included a refresher in each of the lessons to help you learn them one by one. Take this opportunity to refresh your memory one more time as we go through the list.

1. Spirit of wisdom and revelation. Who comes against it? (spirit of Jezebel)

2. Spirit of truth. Who comes against it? (Balaam — spirit of falsehood)

3. Spirit of holiness. Who comes against it? (Korah — spirit of rebellion)

4. Spirit of life. Who comes against it? (Cain — spirit of murder)

5. Spirit of sonship. Who comes against it? (spirit of bondage to fear)

6. Spirit of grace. Who comes against it? (spirit of Baal — to steal the bride)

In this lesson we are looking at the Spirit of glory, and the enemy spirit sent as a counterfeit to block the flow of God's Holy Spirit in your life, your family, your work, and your church. This is the most powerful enemy principality, and it is important to take this very seriously. Peter knew this very well. He knew what it was like to be caught up in spiritual warfare. He knew what it was like to be on the losing side in the battle. He knew what it was like to be on the winning side, and all the areas in between losing and winning. It is good at this point to take some powerful advice from Peter.

*"Beloved, do not think it strange concerning the fiery trial which is to try you, as though some strange thing happened to you; but rejoice to the extent that you partake of Christ's sufferings, that when His glory is revealed, you may also be glad with exceeding joy. If you are reproached for the name of Christ, blessed are you, for the **Spirit of glory** and of God rests upon you. On their part He is blasphemed, but on your part He is glorified. But let none of you suffer as a murderer, a thief, an evildoer, or as a busybody in other people's matters. Yet if anyone suffers as a Christian, let him not be ashamed, but let him glorify God in this matter."* (1 Peter 4:12-16)

According to Peter, one of the seven Spirit of God is the Spirit of glory. The Spirit of glory will come at the time of painful trials and suffering to rest on you and turn all of these experiences into joy and blessing. God sends His glory to parade up and down the front lines to inspire, encourage, and strengthen His soldiers, and to instill fear and trembling in the enemy forces. This is a very powerful Spirit and we need to be able to recognize it and flow with it in order to accomplish our God given goals and purposes.

In this lesson, we will be closely examining the work of the Spirit of glory, and gaining knowledge of how He works and how we can work with Him.

Some people have not been introduced to this Spirit and wonder what "glory" means. I believe the simplest definition is that the glory is the weighty manifest presence of God. When you study the glory of God, you see it being made manifest during many critical points in the history of God's people.

*"...indeed it came to pass, when the trumpeters and singers were as one, to make one sound to be heard in praising and thanking the Lord, and when they lifted up their voice with the trumpets and cymbals and instruments of music, and praised the Lord, saying: "For He is good, For His mercy endures forever," that the house, the house of the Lord, was filled with a cloud, so that the priests could not continue ministering because of the cloud; for the glory of the Lord filled the house of God."* (2 Chronicles 5:13b-14)

The Israelites experienced the glory presence of God as a thick cloud which could fill an area and leave people powerless to function in its presence. It is important to note that, when the Spirit of glory shows up, human effort is not needed. The only thing people need to do is fall down before the manifest presence of God and give Him reverent worship.

Does this glory cloud still appear today? This is a very controversial subject in the church today. Some adamantly say that God never manifests himself this way in the church. Others are equally adamant on the other side, and many have personally witnessed this presence of God. Reading the stories of the Azusa Street Revival, many witnesses saw the glory cloud on a daily basis. There are many reports today of the appearance of this cloud during times of intense worship. I have DVDs showing the appearance in four different services during the last few years. I firmly believe that on rare occasions you can see it. I also believe that you can feel the presence. When it comes, the weight of it is so great that you are literally forced to the floor, and when that happens, you can't do anything except wait upon the Lord. It is a strong reminder that when God is in charge, He doesn't need our help. Our God is a consuming fire (Hebrews 12:29) "For our God *is* a consuming fire." We serve the God who answers by fire and is Himself a consuming fire, and when He fills any place great power comes with his presence.

> *"When Solomon had finished praying, fire came down from heaven and consumed the burnt offering and the sacrifices; and the glory of the Lord filled the temple. And the priests could not enter the house of the Lord, because the glory of the Lord had filled the Lord's house. When all the children of Israel saw how the fire came down, and the glory of the Lord on the temple, they bowed their faces to the ground on the pavement, and worshiped and praised the Lord, saying: "For He is good, For His mercy endures forever."* (2 Chronicles 7:1-3)

The manifest presence of God is like a great heaviness or overwhelming power that will literally push you to the ground, and it may hold you there. We see some of this power in the New Testament at the arrest of Jesus. The soldiers sent out to arrest Him were some really rough and tough guys. They were in charge of maintaining discipline and order in the temple, and they were strong enough and powerful enough to do their jobs. But, look at what happened to these tough guys when they were confronted by the glory presence of God as they met Jesus face to face. Jesus asked them who they were looking for, and they said Jesus of Nazareth. *"Now when He said to them, 'I am He,' they drew back and fell to the ground."* (John 18:6) When these rough tough guys encountered the glory presence in Jesus, they fell back on the ground. It is that powerful. You may be wondering what this has to do with the glory of God. I wonder how many of you know that Jesus is God's glory. Jesus is God's glory dwelling among us, and He is sustaining all things with his power.

*"The Son is the radiance of God's glory and the exact representation of his being, sustaining all things by his powerful word. After he had provided purification for sins, he sat down at the right hand of the Majesty in heaven."* (Hebrews 1:3, NIV)

Jesus is the glory of God, and the glory of God dwelt in Jesus. When He came to our world, He carried this glory to us. He then imparted that glory to us. I want to take this one step further. So, I ask you to listen carefully to Psalm 26:8, *"I love the house where you live, O Lord, the place where your glory dwells."* According to this passage, "Where does God's glory dwell?" Answer: In the Temple!

Now add to that thought the fact that you are the temple of God! *"Do you not know that you are the temple of God and that the Spirit of God dwells in you?"* (1 Corinthians 3:16) Where did Paul say the glory dwells? Answer: In you! Since you are the temple of God and the glory dwells in the temple, then you must realize that the glory dwells in you. You don't have to go on some long journey or great quest to find the glory of God. It is in you! This is good news. For many it is just too good to accept. They have bought into a very low image of who they are in Christ and simply cannot accept that the glory of God could possibly dwell in them.

From the earliest words we have from God, we are told that we have been created in His image. We are told that we are to have dominion over the earth and subdue it. We are told by the Word of God that He created humans to exist at a high level. People doubting these words have misrepresented God's Word to say something other than the truth, because the truth is just too wonderful. Listen to David's affirmation in Psalm 8:

*"What is man that You are mindful of him, and the son of man that You visit him? For You have made him a little lower than the angels, and You have crowned him with glory and honor."* (Psalm 8:4-5)

A very important word in this passage has been mistranslated. In reality, this is not what David wrote. He wrote *"You have made him a little lower than Elohim."* Elohim is the first name for God in the Bible. The translators were afraid to rend it as it was given. The reason God is able to crown us with glory and honor is that He created us that way: not lower than the angels, but lower than Himself. He intended for us to share His glory — to literally be crowned with it. The enemy does not want you to know this. He has used fear to block this Word from you. However in almost every modern translation, the footnotes affirm this truth. You have been created by God to carry His glory, and you don't have to make it on someone else' experience. It's in you!

We fall short of God's plan and destiny for our lives when we fail to see this. Some have told me that we can't affirm this without getting into a spirit of pride. I strongly disagree with this notion. There is nothing like the manifest presence of God to make you totally aware of the gap between who you are and who He is. There is no pride in carrying this glory. There is only humility and the fear of the Lord. The enemy has deceived the church into failing to carry the glory of God into the world. But, the truth is that the glory of God is to be in you and radiate out from you. I recommend that you carefully study the meaning of the following passage of scripture.

*"But we all, with unveiled face, beholding as in a mirror the glory of the Lord, are being transformed into the same image from glory to glory, just as by the Spirit of the Lord."* (2 Corinthians 3:18)

Think about it for a moment! What do you see when you look in a mirror? You may see a variety of backgrounds as you look into different mirrors in various locations. But, there is one constant. When you look into a mirror, you see yourself. Paul is telling you that when you see yourself in the mirror, you should be seeing the glory of the Lord. You are supposed to be in the process of being transformed into the same image as the Lord as you go from "glory to glory, just as by the Spirit of the Lord." Which Spirit of the Lord is referenced here? It is the Spirit of glory. When you see yourself in a mirror, you should say, "There is the glory of God!" If you are having trouble with this, study this scripture over and over and practice saying, "I am the glory of God! When I look at myself in a mirror, I see the glory of the Lord!" Keep saying it until you are comfortable with it, and then continue to say it until it is stored in your heart.

If you can't get to the place where you realize where the glory of the Lord resides, you will always be a victim of the devil. If you can't get to the place in your spirit where you know with certainty that the Spirit of glory resides in you, the enemy will fill that void with his counterfeit spirit sent to steal your self-image, kill your life of authority in the Spirit, and destroy your destiny.

## THE ENEMY ALWAYS COMES AGAINST THE SPIRIT OF GLORY

There is a principality (a prince demon with many sub-ordinate demons) who will come against you to rob you of the glory presence of God. His main work is to veil your eyes through his deceptive words to you. He will bring up past mistakes and failures to make you feel unworthy. He will bring up your family history to make it seem unlikely that God would use someone like you. You must remember that the devil is a liar and the father of all lies. He is constantly telling you little lies and asking questions to raise your doubts and fears. Don't listen to him!

> *"But even if our gospel is veiled, it is veiled to those who are perishing, whose minds the god of this age has blinded, who do not believe, lest the light of the gospel of the glory of Christ, who is the image of God, should shine on them."* (2 Corinthians 4:3-4)

There is a saying in the Army that "the lowest form of human existence is a barracks thief." A barracks thief is someone who is part of your team and lives in the same building where you live. While he pretends to be your friend and assures you that he is trustworthy, in fact he is plotting to steal from you when you are not watching. The enemy loves to find people with that kind of deceptive and dishonest spirit. The enemy is always looking for someone on the inside of your group so that he can use their weaknesses and character defects against you. He sends a very powerful spirit to do this work, because he knows how much damage he can cause through the betrayal of a friend. He went after Judas, and he will go after you through people in your group whom you believe to be your friends.

In his first epistle, John tells us about those from our group who have been enlisted by the enemy to damage the gospel of the glory of God in Jesus Christ. John had already seen many people who had been used by the enemy and were acting as antichrists. He recognized and stated clearly that these people had gone out from the church, but had never really committed their lives to Christ.

> *"Little children, it is the last hour; and as you have heard that the Antichrist is coming, even now many antichrists have come, by which we know that it is the last hour. They went out from us, but they were not of us; for if they had been of us, they would have continued with us; but they went out that they might be made manifest, that none of them were of us."* (1 John 2:18-19)

John identifies them as any who did not confess that Jesus Christ came in the flesh. Those who do not confess Jesus Christ are not of God, and are influenced by or possessed by the spirit of Antichrist. John affirms that this spirit is already in the world. By this denial that Jesus came in the flesh we see a direct attack on the Spirit of glory manifest in the person of Jesus. As we saw in Hebrews 1:3, *"The Son is the radiance of God's glory and the exact representation of his being,"* The spirit of Antichrist denies this fact.

> *"By this you know the Spirit of God: Every spirit that confesses that Jesus Christ has come in the flesh is of God, and every spirit that does not confess that Jesus Christ has come in the flesh is not of God. And this is the spirit of the Antichrist, which you have heard was coming, and is now already in the world."* (1 John 4:2-3)

In the last days, the Antichrist will be an agent of Satan to carry out his plans to kill the saints of God. In Revelation, John sees Satan as a seven headed dragon who deceived one third of the angels in heaven to follow him in a rebellion against God.

His ability to deceive this large number of angels attests to his skill at deception.

*"And another sign appeared in heaven: behold, a great, fiery red dragon having seven heads and ten horns, and seven diadems on his heads. His tail drew a third of the stars of heaven and threw them to the earth. And the dragon stood before the woman who was ready to give birth, to devour her Child as soon as it was born."* (Revelation 12:3-4)

Because of his rebellion against God, the devil was cast out of heaven along with his angel followers. He had been able to deceive as many as one third of all the angels in heaven to join him in this very foolish rebellion against God.

*"So the great dragon was cast out, that serpent of old, called the Devil and Satan, who deceives the whole world; he was cast to the earth, and his angels were cast out with him."* (Revelation 12:9)

Please bear with me as I point out clearly the identity of the principality which comes against the Spirit of glory. The Antichrist is strongly associated with the dragon in Revelation.

*"Then I stood on the sand of the sea. And I saw a beast rising up out of the sea, having seven heads and ten horns, and on his horns ten crowns, and on his heads a blasphemous name. Now the beast which I saw was like a leopard, his feet were like the feet of a bear, and his mouth like the mouth of a lion. The dragon gave him his power, his throne, and great authority. And I saw one of his heads as if it had been mortally wounded, and his deadly wound was healed. And all the world marveled and followed the beast. So they worshiped the dragon*

*who gave authority to the beast; and they worshiped the beast, saying, "Who is like the beast? Who is able to make war with him?"* (Revelation 13:1-4)

The spirit which comes against the Spirit of glory is the manifest presence of the devil in the person of the Antichrist. The principality behind the Antichrist is the spirit of Leviathan. Leviathan is mentioned repeatedly in the scriptures, and Isaiah makes clear that the spirit of Leviathan and the dragon in the sea are one and the same spirit.

*"In that day the LORD with his sore and great and strong sword shall punish leviathan the piercing serpent, even leviathan that crooked serpent; and he shall slay the dragon that is in the sea."* (Isaiah 27:1, KJV)

It is important to note that Leviathan is referred to here as *"the dragon that is in the sea."* Compare Isaiah's reference to Leviathan with the emergence of the Antichrist from the sea who was given the dragon's power, throne, and authority. In this last hour, along with many antichrists there are many false prophets. All of them deny that Jesus (God's radiant glory) came in the flesh. They attempt to counterfeit the Spirit of glory with this terrible spirit of the dragon.

The many references to Leviathan give us a great deal of data about his character, capabilities, and standard means of operating. An examination of his attributes helps us to understand what we are dealing with when Leviathan comes against us. Various translations have referred to him as a piercing, coiling, twisted, winding, crooked, fleeing, and gliding serpent. From these various descriptions, we get a good idea of the methods he uses against those who have received the Spirit of glory. He twists everything to accomplish his crooked and deceitful plans.

He is an expert at twisting words and bringing confusion into the body of Christ. When this spirit is operating in a group, things will soon get so twisted that no one knows what is really going on. The Spirit of glory brings the radiant light of Christ to clarify God's word and God's plans. Leviathan tries to block (or at least hinder) the Spirit's work by bringing confusion into everything and everyone.

In Genesis, Satan is a serpent who talked to Adam and Eve. He was able to deceive them by twisting what God had said to them. They fell for it because he deceived them into thinking they could become equal with God. This same enemy tried to twist God's Word with Jesus, but it didn't work. Jesus did not claim equality with God, but remained obedient even to death on the cross.

If the enemy was able to deceive Adam and Eve by twisting God's Word, you have to know that he will try to do the same with you. Any time you find yourself trying to twist the meaning of God's Word to support your will and purpose or your doctrinal positions instead of accepting God's will and purpose, Leviathan is at work.

As an army chaplain, I provided marriage counseling for hundreds if not thousands of couples during almost 30 years on active duty. I had to deal with the spirit of Leviathan working in almost every couple coming in for marital counseling. As each of the two individuals attempted to explain what had happened it seemed as if they were reporting two entirely different events. As they worked on issues in the office, it was clear that all their words to one another were twisted and confused. Neither of them was able to clearly express their feelings or accurately hear the words of their marital partners.

You could sit and watch the words being twisted somewhere between the tongue of one and the ear of the other. They would usually hear something completely different from what was said. With each statement, the confusion and twisting became more pronounced. It was necessary to stop them, establish new ways of expressing themselves and monitor it for clarity; sentence by sentence. The spirit of Leviathan is a powerful and destructive spirit. I have seen this twisting spirit destroy many relationships and cause unimaginable pain to those who were being oppressed by it in their marriages.

I have seen the same spirit at work in the church. Elder and Deacon Boards seem particularly vulnerable to this enemy spirit. As various members attempt to get their ideas, plans, and programs approved, the other members move into "attack mode" as if an enemy spy had entered their midst. The longer issues are discussed the greater the confusion. There have been many church splits brought about because the members were unable to get control back from this spirit. This is the enemy's primary plan for believers and the church. The enemy can effectively block everything the church plans to accomplish by bringing about a church split. It can take years for a church to recover and get started again.

When the Spirit of glory comes into a church body and people begin to experience the manifest presence of God, lives begin to change and the church may literally explode with growth both in the quantity of people and the quality of spiritual growth. When this happens, the spirit of Leviathan moves in and begins twisting and confusing words spoken between church members, church leaders, and pastors. People become supersensitive to every potential offense and overreact to every situation. How many church splits have been caused by this spirit? How many church movements have been hindered or stopped by the spirit of Leviathan?

When I was stationed in Korea, I would often be called in the middle of the night to go to the Military Police Station and visit with soldiers in the "D-cell." This was a polite way of saying the "drunk tank." After providing ministry to someone for several hours, I would come out and make my way back to my room and hopefully get another hour or two of sleep. When I was called to make these visits, it was usually with urgency, and I would not shave or spend time with my appearance. On several occasions, I was seen early in the morning coming out of the "D-cell" looking like that. Rumors would quickly spread that I had spent the night locked up. As people talked about this, the words became more and more twisted. Some of the church leaders would come to me filled with these twisted words to confront me with my behavior. They were very embarrassed when they learned the truth. They had fallen victim to Leviathan, the twisting spirit and promoted confusion on the base.

When the spirit gets loose in the church, it brings so much confusion that no one seems to understand what is happening. People react to the twisted words instead of checking it out. They make big assumptions and often add even more twisted words as they spread the rumors and gossip. It is as if this spirit blinds us to our normal ability to reason and think through a situation.

When the spirit of Leviathan is loosed in the church, you must understand some painful facts about dealing with it. You can't reason with it, because every word, regardless of how reasonable it may seem, will be twisted into something which the speakers never intended. Even if you meet with people and talk with them face to face, the truth just can't get through. When this spirit is at work in the people who are open to it, they will believe that a lie is the truth and that the truth is a lie. It is the work of this twisting spirit. It seems to coil around people and they can't think straight or hear what's being said.

*"Can you draw out Leviathan with a hook, or snare his tongue with a line which you lower? Can you put a reed through his nose, or pierce his jaw with a hook? Will he make many supplications to you? Will he speak softly to you? Will he make a covenant with you? Will you take him as a servant forever? Will you play with him as with a bird, or will you leash him for your maidens?*

*Will your companions make a banquet of him? Will they apportion him among the merchants? Can you fill his skin with harpoons, or his head with fishing spears? Lay your hand on him; Remember the battle—Never do it again! Indeed, any hope of overcoming him is false; Shall one not be overwhelmed at the sight of him?"* (Job 41:1-9)

From this biblical description, you can see that it is hopeless to work out a compromise with this spirit. You can't make an agreement (covenant) with it. You can't make it a servant to serve your purposes. Once it is loose in a group, the entire group is headed for destruction. We are warned in Job that you can't play with this spirit, but there are people who love to bring strife and contention in a group. They seem to think they can play with this spirit and use and control it for their own purposes and entertainment. They are sadly mistaken. Paul's advice is to stay away from people who are manifesting this spirit.

*"If anyone teaches otherwise and does not consent to wholesome words, even the words of our Lord Jesus Christ, and to the doctrine which accords with godliness, he is proud, knowing nothing, but is obsessed with disputes and arguments over words, from which come envy, strife, reviling, evil suspicions, useless wranglings of men of corrupt minds and destitute of the truth, who suppose that godliness is a means of gain. From such withdraw yourself."* (1Timothy 6:3-5)

When you fail to heed Paul's advice, you discover, the hard way, that you cannot reason with this spirit. If it offers the hope of peace, don't believe it. It will only take you deeper into battle and cause more damage to the body of Christ. A person with this spirit will act as he wants to resolve an issue, but don't believe it. When you meet with someone manifesting this spirit, everything will get twisted and everyone will leave the meeting in total confusion. The advice of Proverbs 22:10, *"Cast out the scoffer, and contention will leave; Yes, strife and reproach will cease."*

Paul wanted the church in Corinth to realize that if they allowed this twisting spirit to work in their group it would destroy their witness to the world. Who wants to join a group of people who profess love, but are in constant strife and repeatedly splitting over petty differences.

> *"And I, brethren, could not speak to you as to spiritual people but as to carnal, as to babes in Christ. I fed you with milk and not with solid food; for until now you were not able to receive it, and even now you are still not able; for you are still carnal. For where there are envy, strife, and divisions among you, are you not carnal and behaving like mere men?"* (1 Corinthians 3:1-3)

## HOW DO YOU FIGHT AGAINST LEVIATHAN?

The best answer is that you don't fight with Leviathan. No matter what you say, it will get twisted. No matter what you do, it will turn to confusion. You can't reason with him, and you can't bargain with him. You can't make a covenant with him, and you can never trust anything he says. You can't get through his thick skin and you can't do him any real harm. God has made this clear by giving us so many warnings in the Bible. He has also given the Holy Spirit to guide us into all truth. These warnings are part of that body of truth. So, it is very important to pay close attention to the warnings in the scriptures. God asks Job a series of questions and the answer to each of them is, "NO!" I will separate them and provide this answer for reinforcement purposes. Listen to the Lord's advice to Job (see Job 41:1-9)

1. "Can you draw out Leviathan with a hook," NO!
   "Or *snare* his tongue with a line *which* you lower?" NO!
2. "Can you put a reed through his nose," NO!
   "Or pierce his jaw with a hook?" NO!
3. "Will he make many supplications to you?" NO!
   "Will he speak softly to you?" NO!
4. "Will he make a covenant with you?" NO!
   "Will you take him as a servant forever?" NO!
5. "Will you play with him as *with* a bird," NO!
   "Or will you leash him for your maidens?" NO!
6. "Will *your* companions make a banquet of him?" NO!
   "Will they apportion him among the merchants?" NO!
7. "Can you fill his skin with harpoons," NO!
   "Or his head with fishing spears? NO!
8. Lay your hand on him; Remember the battle—Never do it again!
9. Indeed, *any* hope of *overcoming* him is false;
   Shall *one not* be overwhelmed at the sight of him?"

The Lord makes it abundantly clear that none of your regular weapons of spiritual warfare will work with this spirit. You can't bind him or pierce his armor. If you ever go to war with this spirit, you will not forget the pain and suffering which result. Everything you try to say or do will get confused and twisted. It is important to learn the lesson of the Angel Michael,

*"Yet Michael the archangel, in contending with the devil, when he disputed about the body of Moses, dared not bring against him a reviling accusation, but said, "The Lord rebuke you!" But these speak evil of whatever they do not know; and whatever they know naturally, like brute beasts, in these things they corrupt themselves!"* (Jude 1:9-10)

You must learn to let the Lord deal with Leviathan. If you get caught up in making accusations about others whom you believe are operating under the influence of this spirit, you are out of line. We are not to accuse one another. We should have the same fear of the Lord which Michael the archangel has. Remember in scripture, the accuser is Satan. When you get caught up in making accusations, you are doing his work and not the Lord's work. This is one of the greatest weaknesses in the body of Christ. People are constantly making accusations about one another. Friends this should not be, because when we do this, we are actually opening up the way for Leviathan to come in and make a shambles of our church or family.

You must understand that the spirit of Leviathan has two openings into churches and families. The first and primary opening is through a spirit of pride. It is the spirit of pride which is behind accusations. And, the spirit of confusion loves to work in proud people. His job with them is easy, because they think they are the only ones who can get things straightened out. They don't listen to others or see all the sides in the conflict. In their pride, they believe they have the only correct answer. This type of pride makes them blind and vulnerable. Listen to the warning God gave to Job about the consequences of pride:

*"He (Leviathan) beholds every high thing; He is king over all the children of pride."* (Job 41:34)

The second opening for the spirit of Leviathan is through character flaws. People who struggle with guilt or have a poor self-image are very susceptible to being used by the spirit of Leviathan. People who believe they are ugly, resent people who are beautiful. Beautiful people see their own flaws and think they are ugly. Some rich people are driven because they are not rich enough and end up feeling poor. Other rich people feel guilty about having so much and fear that God will send them to hell for hoarding. People who are poor feel helpless and hopeless and resent those who are wealthy. So, this is a problem for almost everyone. And we see over and over that people with low self esteem tend to cope by twisting things about others in order to bring others down to their level. How should you deal with people like this? Instead of blaming them, you need to be aware that the spirit of Leviathan has twisted their thinking. They are blinded to the fact that when God created them, He said, "It is very good!" God has made all of us to be right in His eyes and for His purpose. To Him and for His purposes, we are all rich, beautiful, talented, and of great value.

People with low self esteem just can't grasp this. Proud people tend to believe it about themselves, but don't attribute it to anyone else. Both situations make an easy opening for Leviathan to come in and do his dirty work.

It is also very important to remember that you can't make Leviathan a pet. You can't manipulate him into doing your will. You cannot befriend him. He is confusion, and he twists everything. He does not work for you or with you. He will use you for his purposes. But, you must always remember that his plan is the same as Satan's plan. He wants to steal, kill, and destroy. His ultimate goal is to destroy you. If you try to use him for your purposes, you will be confused when things go well and when they don't go well. You simply cannot get into an "OK" relationship with confusion.

You'll have to turn this battle over to the lord. You don't have the weapons, tactics, or traps necessary to catch him or destroy him. This is the Lord's battle, and we must learn to let Him fight the battle. When Leviathan comes against us, he is actually coming against the Spirit of glory, and God will rise up to deal with him.

*"You broke the heads of Leviathan in pieces, And gave him as food to the people inhabiting the wilderness."* (Psalm 74:14)

The enemy will never be able to stop the Spirit of glory. It is the Spirit of glory who will ultimately defeat all these wicked spirits. The Lord will not let the enemy block His plan. It is God's plan and purpose to send His glory among us, and His plans will not fail unless we refuse to receive the Spirit of glory. I like to meditate on Paul's question to the Romans.

*"What if he did this to make the riches of his glory known to the objects of his mercy, whom he prepared in advance for glory"* (Romans 9:23, NIV)

Notice that Paul is saying that you were created in advance for glory. It was part of God's plan from the beginning to make you in such a way that He could deposit the Spirit of glory in you. You were created to be God's temple where His glory will dwell. It is God's plan to put His glory into you, and let it radiate out from you to bless others.

Leviathan doesn't like that. So, he tries to twist things until you don't think you are worthy. He wants you to believe that it has not happened and will not happen. He wants to make you think that it is somehow wrong for you to believe that God's glory could be in you. I have heard so many people confess this by saying, "There is no glory in people." And they claim this to be true in order to ensure that you cannot glory in yourself. It is true that you don't glory in yourself, but you better glory in God. If you want to be true to what Jesus taught and what the scriptures say, you need to be open to the presence of God's Spirit of glory in you. Don't even think about going into battle without the Spirit of glory in you!

Jesus clearly knew His purpose in this dispensation of glory. He said, *"I have given them the glory that you gave me, that they may be one as we are one:"* (John 17:22, NIV) Jesus gave us the same glory that God gave to Him. To be obedient to Jesus, we need to be living in that glory and letting that glory flow through us. It is closely tied to that concept of rivers of living water flowing through us. This is the reality which Paul spoke of when he said we should see God's glory when we look in a mirror. Every day that glory should be brighter as we go from glory to glory even into the image of Christ.

We know by now that the spirit of Leviathan is determined to hinder if not totally block that flow of God's glory in us. But, take heart saints of God. God has a powerful weapon to use against Leviathan.

*"In that day the* LORD *with His severe sword (severe sword sounds pretty awful doesn't it), great and strong, will punish Leviathan the fleeing serpent, Leviathan that twisted serpent; and He will slay the reptile that is in the sea."* (Isaiah 27:1)

We see in this passage that God has a mighty sword which Isaiah describes as severe, great, and strong. We have the sword of the Spirit (the Word of God). God has a sword which is infinitely greater than what has been given to us. No weak, wimpy, half-hearted warrior can ever straighten out a spirit of confusion. It takes a skilled and powerful swordsman to deal with this spirit. No proud and arrogant person can clear up Leviathan's confusion. It will take God Himself to bring down this seven headed dragon, Leviathan.

When I played high school football, we played against some teams which were actually coached to create injuries to the opposing team. One of their tricks was to have two players dive down and hold your feet to the ground while another hit you from the side to dislocate your knees. They had many other strategies to create other injuries. Sometimes they were so focused on causing injuries that their focus on the game was lost. In my particular year group all of the players were several inches taller than those in the years before us or after us. In a very small town, the average height of our team was over six feet and two inches. When we played against those teams which had been coached to play dirty, I made a deal with the Fullback. At the snap of the ball, I would stand up and look very vulnerable. This drew the other team to come after me. But, I would suddenly drop to the ground, and while their eyes were on me, the fullback (6'2" and 245 lbs) would dive across my back and take them out. What they had not seen while I was standing up was that he had taken an 8 yard running start to reach my position. He had built up a lot of momentum, and when he hit them it was a devastating blow. It was so shocking for the other team that they stopped lining up to cause injuries. It only took a couple of lessons for them to learn that their strategy was no longer working.

As I thought about how we can deal with Leviathan, this memory came back to me. We need to learn to duck down and let God deal with Leviathan. While Leviathan is distracted by our apparent vulnerability, we just fall face down and let the Spirit of glory come across our back and render a devastating blow to this wicked and vicious spirit. Make room for the Spirit of glory to dwell in you. Don't hide from it or deny it. Remember the promise in Isaiah 58:8b (NIV), "The glory of the Lord shall be your rear guard." We need to step aside and pray for the wisdom of God. We need to make room for the Spirit of glory to dwell in us, because when the Spirit of glory fills a place, there's no room for confusion.

Remember in earlier lessons we looked at how the Special Forces fight, back to back, firing on the enemy in all directions. Back to back, they are in a defensive posture to cover their fellow soldiers. Back to back, they are not firing on each other, but concentrating the fire on the enemy. This style of fighting makes it difficult for the enemy to get into the camp where he can do too much damage. All of the enemy spirits want to get into the camp and attack from within. And, that is what Leviathan does. He finds someone who is weak or has an unresolved character defect and uses that person against the group.

He wants to create confusion and deceive us into attacking one another. We must always remember Paul's warning:

*"Finally, my brethren, be strong in the Lord and in the power of His might. Put on the whole armor of God, that you may be able to stand against the wiles of the devil. For we do not wrestle against flesh and blood, but against principalities, against powers, against the rulers of the darkness of this age, against spiritual hosts of wickedness in the heavenly places. Therefore take up the whole armor of God, that you may be able to withstand in the evil day, and having done all, to stand."* (Ephesians 6:10-13 )

We must never lose sight of the fact that our battle is against these wicked spirits and not against one another. So, any time we sense this spirit of confusion coming into our families or into our churches, we immediately recognize it, because we have been trained. We are alert and ready. When this spirit comes, we immediately recognize that it is the spirit of Leviathan. Before he can turn us against one another we need to band together to deal with him quickly and effectively.

We need to make a firm choice that we are not going to let this happen in the place where the glory of God dwells. We are determined that this will not happen in the place where the glory of God is working in our lives and we are experiencing the manifest presence of the Lord. We are not going to allow this wicked spirit to block the rivers of living water flowing through us into the world. We will not let him block the presence of God which is literally changing the atmosphere around us as the Spirit of glory is flowing through us.

We must learn that this has to be done together. We are not lone rangers fighting all the battles by ourselves. We are a team and we have learned to be force multipliers by working together. We must learn to stand together, support the pastor, and deal with the enemy spirits. We must agree to do this together, and use the wisdom of the Holy Spirit to keep us focused on the truth. We must stop reacting to Leviathan's wiles, and learn to turn immediately to the Lord. We must stop attacking one another. As soon as confusion moves in, we must learn to say, "Oh no, you don't! We know what is happening here, and we are standing together against the spirit of confusion." We are standing together against all the wicked spirits of this dark world, and we are doing it together in the unity of the Holy Spirit.

I don't know about you, but I love the manifest presence of God. I love to feel His weighty presence and to know that He is present. He is dwelling in each of us who are created to hold His glory. He is dwelling in each of the temples He has created for this purpose. I love what happens when this powerful Spirit of God comes into our midst and begins to bring glory into everyone and into everything we are doing. I don't want to lose that! What we must do is agree together that we will stop reacting to Leviathan. We will understand his tricks, and not allow ourselves to be caught up in the confusion. We need to watch each other's back, and when we see the twisting begin, we agree to say, "Oh, No you don't!" All you have to do is resist. The Lord will do all the real fighting with His seven Spirits. Remember the promise in James 4:7, *"Therefore submit to God. Resist the devil and he will flee from you."* Get into the practice of praying James 4:7 daily. I modified it like this:

Father God, I submit to you spirit, soul, and body; all that I am and all that I ever hope to be; all that I have and all that I ever will have. I resist the devil, and in accordance with your Word and in the mighty name of Jesus, he must flee and take all his works with him. In Jesus' name! Amen!

If you can take these simple steps, you will be armed when Leviathan shows up. You are armed with the Spirit of glory; the manifest presence of God. Let the Holy Spirit come in and remove the confusion. Remember the goodness of God and place all your trust in Him. Amen!

*"Oh, how great is Your goodness, which You have laid up for those who fear You, which You have prepared for those who trust in You In the presence of the sons of men! You shall hide them in the secret place of Your presence from the plots of man; You shall keep them secretly in a pavilion from the strife of tongues."* (Psalm 31:19-20)

## PRAYER TO RECEIVE THE SPIRIT OF GLORY

Father God, we are submitting to you today; spirit, soul, and body! We submit everything to you. And, Father God, we stand against — we resist — the enemy. We are standing in faith on your Word. We are standing in faith on the powerful name of Jesus Christ. We are standing together on the promise that when we submit to you and resist the enemy, he must flee from us. So, Lord God, we ask today that you pour out the Spirit of glory. Let your Spirit of glory come into our midst! Let your Spirit of glory come into each of our hearts! Let your Spirit of glory be manifest in our lives, and in our service!

Father God, we just want that glory to flow and we want to be standing in the flow of your manifest presence. Thank you for the Spirit of wisdom and revelation; the Spirit of truth; the Spirit of holiness; the Spirit of life, the Spirit of sonship, the Spirit of grace, and the Spirit of glory! Father God, we just submit now and receive these seven powerful Spirits to empower us to stand for you in faith. Father God, we ask all these things in the glorious name of Yeshua ha Messiach. Amen and Amen!

## ADDITONAL SCRIPTURES FOR FUTHER STUDY

Revelation 15:8 (NKJV), "The temple was filled with smoke from the glory of God and from His power, and no one was able to enter the temple till the seven plagues of the seven angels were completed."

1 Thessalonians 2:11-12 (NIV), "For you know that we dealt with each of you as a father deals with his own children, encouraging, comforting and urging you to live lives worthy of God, who calls you into his kingdom and glory."

Luke 21:27 (NIV), "At that time they will see the Son of Man coming in a cloud with power and great glory."

Hosea 4:7 (NIV), "The more the priests increased, the more they sinned against me; they exchanged their Glory for something disgraceful."

## NOTES

# SUMMARY

I have presented this material in several training settings over the past two years, and in the process of teaching the Lord has revealed many things to me! Early on, I made the mistake of talking too much about the enemy and his capabilities. I've noticed that most people get very interested when we talk about demons and demonic activity. There seems to be something exciting about them. I believe this unholy attraction is behind the highly profitable production of so many movies about ghosts, demons, possession, and the devil. People seem to be drawn to these things, and then as they see more and more they start to become frightened by them. Too much fear can be paralyzing and can result in a debilitating cowardice which displeases and dishonors our Father God.

Another thing I have learned is that it is a mistake to attribute too much power to the enemy. This is the same mistake the ten Hebrew spies made when they gave their status report on the "promised land." Their report produced so much fear in the people that the entry into the "promised land" was delayed for forty hears. As a result of receiving this understanding from the Lord, I began to make some changes in the conferences where this is taught. Now, I like to begin each training event by making some declarations.

First and foremost, it is important to remember what an awesome God we serve. He is omnipotent (all powerful)! He is the mighty one who created the heavens and the earth and has authority and dominion over everything in the created order and in heaven! There is absolutely nothing too difficult for Him! He is omnipresent (in all places at the same time). He is omniscient (knows all things). There is no power in heaven or on earth that can stop Him! He is the star breathing God who created and is still creating. He speaks things into being, and by His Word everything is set in order. His words never return to Him void.

He is, at the same time, all that each of His many names proclaim. I am listing a few representative names for our awesome God and what they mean. Part of these were listed in a previous lesson. However, I believe that repetition is the key to remembering and owning the promises of God. We need to store them in our hearts in order to have them available as the "sword of the Spirit" later. Remember: "*So then faith comes by hearing, and hearing by the word of God.*" (Romans 10:17) Speak them! Proclaim them! Decree them. Believe that He is all this and so very much more!

| | |
|---|---|
| ADONAI... | "Lord" over everything |
| EL-ELYON, | "The most high God" |
| ELOHIM... | "The God of power and might!" |
| EL-OLAM | "The everlasting God" |
| EL-ROI | "The strong one who sees" |
| EL-SHADDAI | "God of the mountains - God Almighty" |
| JEHOVAH-JIREH | "The Lord will provide" |
| JEHOVAH-NISSI | "The Lord our banner" |
| JEHOVAH-RAPHA | "The Lord our healer" |
| JEHOVAH-ROHI | "The Lord my shepherd" |
| JEHOVAH-SABBAOTH | "The Lord of Hosts" |
| JEHOVAH-SHALOM | "The Lord is peace" |
| JEHOVAH-SHAMMAH | "The Lord who is present" |

JEHOVAH-YAHWEH      "God of our salvation"
YAHWEH                  "The God who is"

There are not enough names to describe Him, His character, His power, His glory, or His majesty! We have a gigantic, almighty, and every present God who is fully capable of accomplishing all things in His purpose and for our purpose. There is no force on earth or in heaven which can separate us from the love of God in Christ Jesus. Study, meditate on, and get the promises of Romans 8 into your heart.

> *"What then shall we say to these things? If God is for us, who can be against us? He who did not spare His own Son, but delivered Him up for us all, how shall He not with Him also freely give us all things? Who shall bring a charge against God's elect? It is God who justifies. Who is he who condemns? It is Christ who died, and furthermore is also risen, who is even at the right hand of God, who also makes intercession for us. Who shall separate us from the love of Christ? Shall tribulation, or distress, or persecution, or famine, or nakedness, or peril, or sword? As it is written: "For Your sake we are killed all day long; We are accounted as sheep for the slaughter." Yet in all these things we are more than conquerors through Him who loved us. For I am persuaded that neither death nor life, nor angels nor principalities nor powers, nor things present nor things to come, nor height nor depth, nor any other created thing, shall be able to separate us from the love of God which is in Christ Jesus our Lord."* (Romans 8:31-40)

If you are tempted to fear, remember: 2 Timothy 1:7, *"For God has not given us a spirit of fear, but of power and of love and of a sound mind."* The Bible reminds us over 328 times that we should not be afraid. We should be courageous and bold because we have the awesome power of God with us. It was released through these seven Spirits of God which the Lord Jesus sent out into all the world. These seven Spirits also remind us that God is always with us and for us, even to the end of this age.

We have a mighty, awesome, and wise God who is infinitely greater than any other being. We also have this tiny little devil who is a nuisance from time to time. But, next to God the devil is truly a nobody.

> *"It is enough for a disciple that he be like his teacher, and a servant like his master. If they have called the master of the house Beelzebub, how much more will they call those of his household! Therefore do not fear them. For there is nothing covered that will not be revealed, and hidden that will not be known."* (Matthew 10:25-26)

Beelzebub, lord of the flies, is a nuisance like a fly which continues to buzz around you at a picnic. We deal with him to stop the nuisance, but we must not attribute power and authority to him. He only has the power and authority we give to him. Remember what Jesus said in Luke 10:18-19, *"And He said to them, 'I saw Satan fall like lightning from heaven. Behold, I give you the authority to trample on serpents and scorpions, and over all the power of the enemy, and nothing shall by any means hurt you.'"* We must learn to keep our eyes fixed on Jesus; operate in the power of the Seven Spirits of God; and take authority over all the power of the enemy.

You died with Christ! You were raised with Him and seated in heavenly places! You are positioned to return with Christ to rule and reign for a thousand years. Don't let the lies and deception of a dead spirit mislead you into fear. Remember that the cowardly and the unbelieving are first on the list of those who go into the lake of fire.

*"And He said to me, 'It is done! I am the Alpha and the Omega, the Beginning and the End. I will give of the fountain of the water of life freely to him who thirsts. He who overcomes shall inherit all things, and I will be his God and he shall be My son. But the cowardly, unbelieving, abominable, murderers, sexually immoral, sorcerers, idolaters, and all liars shall have their part in the lake which burns with fire and brimstone, which is the second death."* (Revelation 21:6-8)

We are called to be a part of the mighty army of God. It is time for all of us to sign up and be part of the great end-time special forces of our Lord. It is time to learn how to effectively wage spiritual warfare utilizing the mighty forces of God's seven Spirits. So, put on the full armor of God and show up for the battle. Warriors run toward the sound of the battle and not away from it. You are called to be like one of David's mighty men with a face like a lion as well as the heart of lion. We are going from glory to glory every day into the very image of the Lion of the Tribe of Judah, the King of kings, and the Lord of lords. May you be fully equipped as you receive the impartation and anointing available through these seven mighty Spirits!

# APPENDIX A

# Carl Von Clausewitz: 9 Principles of War

Around the time of Napoleon, Carl Von Clausewitz, a brilliant military expert wrote the book, "On War." In this book, he identified nine critically important principles of war. These principles were so well thought out and wisely presented that they are still used in officer training around the world. These principles are:

1. **Mass**: mass your forces for maximum power to defeat the enemy.

2. **Objective**: Clearly identify the primary objective and stay focused on it until it is achieved.

3. **Offensive**: Rather than taking a defensive position, seize the initiative and take the fight to the enemy using surprise where possible.

4. **Maneuver**: Continuously move your forces to positions advantageous to your operations.

5. **Unity of Command**: All forces must be under the command of one single leadership element.

6. **Security**: Protect and defend your positions from enemy infiltration or invasion which would give them the advantage.

7. **Simplicity**: Plans must be simple, clear, and understood at all levels to insure the focus will remain on the primary objective in the fog battle.

8. **Surprise**: Take the battle to the enemy when he least expects it and is least prepared to defend against your assault.

9. **Economy of Force**: Properly align you forces for maximum impact in all areas of the battle.

# DIVORCE DECREE FROM BAAL

## THE HIGHEST COURT
## OF THE KINGDOM OF GOD

**IN RE THE MARRIAGE OF:**
THE PEOPLE OF GOD,
      Plaintiff,

vs.

THE PRINCIPALITY OF BAAL
      Defendant,

### DECREE OF DIVORCE*

    This matter comes on for hearing before the Supreme Judge of the Highest Court of the Kingdom of God on the petition of The People of God seeking a Decree of Divorce from The Principality of Baal, the Defendant in this matter.

The Court finds:

1. The Plaintiff's assertions are fully substantiated:

   a. That this marriage was entered into by the Plaintiff based on lies and deceit by the Defendant, and

   b. That Plaintiff relied on fraudulent inducements and enticements by the Defendant, which Defendant had neither the intention or ability to deliver

2. The Plaintiff renounces any and all right, claim or interest in any possession jointly acquired with the Defendant during this Marriage, and that Plaintiff is entitled to have sole right, claim, and interest, in and to all the gifts, possessions and inheritance from Plaintiff's Father, and the Defendant is to be and forever barred from the title, control, or use of any such gifts, possessions or inheritance.

3. That all offspring of the marriage have been still born or have had viability for only brief periods and were either destroyed by the Defendant or were so infected by sickness attributed to the Defendant's condition that no life remained in them.

4. The Plaintiff repudiates any and all joint claims with the Defendant, and requests this court to sever all relationships with the Defendant of any nature, however and whenever such occurred, and seeks enforcement by this Court of Plaintiff's desire to be known by no other name that that given by Plaintiff's Father.

5. The Plaintiff also seeks an everlasting restraining order against the Defendant so as to keep the Defendant away from all persons or property belonging to the Plaintiff.

## THE JUDGEMENT

WHEREFORE, this Court being fully advised in the evidence does find for the Plaintiff and against the Defendant in all matters material to the Plaintiff's Petition of Divorce, and does by this decree grant the Plaintiff a Divorce and all requests set forth above.

That being the Order of this Court, from and after this date, so shall it be.

## THE SUPREME JUDGE

* Composed by Dr. Jerry L. Mash (Oklahoma Apostolic Prayer Network)

**For Additional Information:**
Dr. John Benefiel, Apostolic Coordinator
Heartland Apostolic Prayer Network
P.O. Box 720006
Oklahoma City, OK 73172
Phone: 405-943-2484
Fax: 405-749-0345
Website: www.hapn.us or www.cotr.tv
Email: assistant@hapn.us

## PLAINTIFF'S DECREE

Through the finding of the Court for the Plaintiff, the Plaintiff now makes the following Decree:

On _____, I, _____
_____, do hereby decree on behalf of my family and our future generations that:

1. We no longer have any ties with Baal-hamon. We are Tithers and Givers and therefore we are rightful heirs to the Great Transfer of Wealth to the Church.

2. We no longer have any ties with Baal-berith. We are now free to choose to remarry Jehovah, the only true God, and be in an everlasting covenant and relationship with Him.

3. We reclaim our sexual innocence and purity. We walk in holiness and we reject every form of sexual perversion, homosexuality, and sexual immorality.

4. We are for the next generation. We are for the Unborn's Right to Life. We will pray and support the next generation to see God's covenantal purposes fulfilled in them.

5. We no longer have any ties with any form of witchcraft and occult spirits.

**THE PLAINTIFF**

_____

_____

\* Composed by Dr. Jerry L. Mash (Oklahoma Apostolic Prayer Network)

## For Additional Information:
Dr. John Benefiel, Apostolic Coordinator
Heartland Apostolic Prayer Network
P.O. Box 720006
Oklahoma City, OK 73172
Phone: 405-943-2484
Fax: 405-749-0345
Website: www.hapn.us or www.cotr.tv
Email: assistant@hapn.us

MK 4:24 the measure you use

Eph 6
unity Glory

2013· ONe voice

pg 41 93,94
pg 43
pg 58,59
pg 63,65
pg 67,69 prayer
pg 72 pg 89
pg 90 91
9232 - James Durham
9363 -

CPSIA information can be obtained at www.ICGtesting.com
Printed in the USA
243478LV00002B/7/P